To JoAnn

Thank you for your support + encouragement
throughout the years.

Love You

The
JOYFUL SOUND

Jennifer Rundlett

7/24/16

JENNIFER RUNDLETT

The
JOYFUL SOUND

Reflections on the Life of Christ in Art & Music

www.godthruthearts.com

To my mother Jewell Clarkston,

with loving thanks,

who is still listening,

learning and telling the story.

CONTENTS

PREFACE

HOW TO USE THIS BOOK

THIS BOOK IS MEANT TO BE A GUIDE through many different experiences of the arts with the intention of creating a deeper intimacy with Jesus. Because of this, some brief words about how to approach the arts seem appropriate.

Since the publication of my first book, I have traveled across the country meeting new friends and fellow art lovers. I have enjoyed hearing of their diverse approaches to the meditations in *My Dancing Day*. One dear brother, excited and hungry for artistic experiences in scripture, read quickly through my book and then committed to reading the book again at a slower pace during the Advent season with his wife, while my mother-in-law used the book each week as she prepared her thoughts for the celebration of Mass. Both are wonderful! As it is my ultimate mission to show the ecumenical nature of works of art, individual creative use of the book to fit your lifestyle and church tradition is a must, and a choice I highly admire.

Because this book outlines a method that will be a new experience for many, I have included a few of my recommended tips for optimum use of this book.

I encourage you to begin by setting aside a special time each day for quiet reflection. I still love rising early before the alarm so that I might linger over my morning coffee with some rich spiritual nourishment. However, a different time of day may appeal to you more. The important thing is to create sacred time and space in your day. Allowing yourself time to center your scattered thoughts on things of a spiritual nature will help you approach each chapter with curiosity and attentiveness.

Next, you need to open yourself so that you may release any past interpretations or impressions you have for each of the episodes of Jesus' life. Give yourself permission to go on a voyage of discovery each day. Becoming comfortable with the emptiness is a very important step of the process. The more you become comfortable with the feeling of not knowing, the more you will begin to discover and grow in your spiritual life.

Once you have committed yourself to this, I recommend that you start each chapter by simply looking at the art. Allow yourself to wonder what the artist might be trying to say through their work. Read over the opening verses of the time-honored hymn chosen to introduce the chapter; or you may wish to also read the Bible passages featured within the chapter before reading through the chapter itself. Again, allow yourself to feel emptiness, maybe even admit to feeling dryness towards the chosen texts. When you allow yourself this kind of preparation, I believe you experience greater benefit from the reading of each chapter, as you use these works of art and music as a medium for new insight and a deeper understanding of Jesus' story.

Each chapter contains examples and recommendations of art and music you can explore; however, as you move through the book you will find the approach to each chapter varies. This is because as I worked through the different episodes in the life of Christ, I found that each of them called for a unique treatment. Some will have a step-by-step meditation that corresponds to a great painting, as in Chapter Five with the story of Jesus visiting Mary and Martha's house. Other chapters, such as the exploration of the Seven Last Words of Christ on the Cross in Chapter Seven, will have a musical emphasis. In every case, my thoughts are only one way of viewing a specific passage of scripture, and only meant as a beginning for your further reflections. You have my permission to explore further, and indeed, this is the intent: to encourage you toward self-reflection. This is the beauty of the arts; there is not one answer or one way to enter a scene, and it is my hope that you will become more comfortable with thinking of paintings and music as personal enrichment and a source of the Divine.

To give you more time to familiarize yourself with an artist, you will find I have added a section called Descant to most of the chapters. This is a musical term that means a melodic line added to a sacred hymn, usually occurring as the congregation sings the final verse. As a flutist, I am frequently asked to play the descant, and I enjoy flying above the rest of the voices, embellishing the music with a grand statement at the end. In this way, these additional materials are meant to give you an extra elaboration to make your heart soar as you finish the chapter.

For those of you who might be using the book to lead a class or develop a sermon series, in each chapter I have included additional art recommendations that will help you become more familiar with each artist, and a list of available arts resources. You can type the name of the artist and the title of the painting into a search engine to find art that is in the public domain, in places such as WikiArt, Wikimedia Commons, and Google Art Project.

To support discussion, an appendix called Questions for Group Reflection and Discussion has been included in the back of the book, organized by chapter. Again, these are only meant as a way to "prime the pump," so to speak, and can be reformulated or supplemented with your own questions and scriptures to suit the needs of your individual classes.

Finally, and I highly encourage this: whether you are working individually or in a group, take the time to journal your thoughts each day. Use the Journal and Reflect sections to begin this process. Allow yourself time to jot down ideas or quotes you found surprising or interesting each day. Notice things that are calling to you or attracting you. You can also use the Devotional Prayers in each chapter to direct or help begin journaling your thoughts. As you take time to do this, I am confident you will be led by the Spirit to new insights about familiar stories, or "unpack" certain time-honored church vocabulary and traditions that will bring you to greater intimacy with Jesus. It is my hope that once you become familiar with using art and music in your quiet times, it will become a practice you will return to time and again throughout your spiritual journey.

There are a great variety of ways to find the music for this book. It matters not if you choose Amazon Prime, iTunes, Spotify; or YouTube; the important thing is that you find a way that is comfortable and reliable, so that you will be able to access the music several times.

I prefer to use Spotify for most of my musical needs. This wonderful site offers a program that you can download safely onto your computer, enabling you to access a wondrous library of music in all genres. Once you have downloaded Spotify, you can type my suggested music into the search engine and easily find the musical selection.

You might also find these selections at your local library, either in person or through the many digital online resources many libraries now offer free to the public. I encourage you to ask your librarian for guidance in this area; you will be amazed at the resources that are close to home. Most of the pieces within this book are just a taste of a much larger work, and so only a doorway into further listening pleasure. Because of this, I have included recommended recordings throughout the book for you to use should you decide to look for the complete works.

Finally, you may also like to watch these pieces being performed, and for this reason I have provided a playlist on YouTube. Type "Jennifer Rundlett A Joyful Sound" into the YouTube search engine to locate the playlist for this book.

INTRODUCTION

COME AND SEE

AS WE BEGIN OUR JOURNEY TOGETHER, I would like to explain my method and motive in writing these meditations. This book is actually the companion to my first book, titled *My Dancing Day: Reflections of the Incarnation in Art and Music*, and it is my intent to continue developing the picture of Jesus that was begun in the pages of those reflections.

If you have not read my first book, no matter, as the story of Jesus is unfolded to us gently every year throughout the liturgical calendar. Whether or not you are currently steeped in these kinds of traditional observations, God's story of love keeps giving birth to new life all around you. It is my hope that this book of reflections will refresh and prepare you for the annual celebrations we hold dear.

Regardless of where you currently place yourself in his story, a reading of Jesus' life is like a reoccurring melody that centers itself on a particular note of the scale. Because of our many church traditions, this note will be different for each of us, and yet it is in finding our way back to the original resonance of Jesus' melody that we make progress in our imitation of Christ. These meditations are written to work as an aid to your greater reflections, helping you to wade into the water at your most comfortable point and to immerse yourself in the art and music depicting Jesus' life.

For me, my first book ended with an upward sweep of optimism and enthusiasm. I was absolutely vibrating with anticipation for the future thanks to my newfound vision of God. Jesus, as I experienced him, was a child dancing all around me and playfully inviting me to join him. It stood to reason, then, that life would forever be filled with abundance. I had cracked the code; I was on my way, and life would eternally be painted with some kind of rose-colored hue. I knew there would be challenges, but the unforeseen bumps in the road would never again throw my cart into the ditch. God was with me, and I was excited to move forward.

But as most of us learn over time, happily ever after only happens in the pages of a fairytale. And life for me became real very quickly. Therefore, it was with a certain amount of hesitation that I approached the writing of this second book. God allows us to walk through difficulties as an important part of our transformation process. I knew this project would be no exception. The desire that pushed me onward, however, was a hope that further meditations on the adult life of Jesus would be a sort of "field guide" for someone longing for a deeper connection to God through developing an intimate picture of Christ.

So how do we get from a picture of Jesus as a child, innocent and playful, to an image of Jesus, the full-grown man?

Further, how do we imagine him as someone who lived as the Son of God, and died so that he might give us life?

Knowing that his life and ministry ultimately lead to the cross sometimes causes us to look away from Jesus' life in its entirety and to focus on the more palatable parts of the story. For myself, I had endeavored to hold on to the attractive, warm, and comfortable parts of his story to the exclusion of the rest, and in doing so I had become like a child myself, trying to hold the light of his story tightly in the palm of my hand. Eager to protect the beauty of my understanding, I began to form a fist around it, presenting a hardness toward anything that risked an opening or change of my view of him.

Always mindful of our ways, God in his wisdom will allow the opening of our hands and our hearts with life-changing events that seem quite difficult to understand at times. It is in these moments that we can feel off-balance as we suddenly realize the fire inside us has died... and that, like a lost child, we have forgotten our way.

These are the times that we can find our deepest connection to God if we remember to turn and really look at the wholeness of Jesus' life and ministry. This book seeks to bring these events into closer perspective by using paintings and music as our source of inspiration.

Within these pages, I have carefully crafted meditations that will bring new insight into a cross-section of episodes in the life of Christ. In this way, you will be practicing a process others have termed *visio divina,* which means "divine seeing," and what I like to refer to as "praying a painting." Using art, and music, as a vehicle to deeper spirituality is a time-honored method practiced worldwide. As we follow in that tradition, these meditations encourage you to awaken your senses to the reading from scripture so that you may connect to the story emotionally. This kind of prayerful listening, regularly practiced, will facilitate hearing God's message in a uniquely personal way as we travel through some of the treasured stories recorded in the gospels. Through prayerful readings of scripture and directed journal exercises, you will find your individual song. When we dare to see our own scars clearly in the wounds of Jesus, we learn to rise up, as he did, and give birth to new life one extraordinary day at a time.

"Come,... and you will see." (John 1:39, NIV) as we begin this journey of transformation toward a greater understanding of the heart of God by looking into the face of Jesus and learning to sing a joyful new song.

PART ONE

HEARING OUR DIVINE CALLING

You, O Lord, keep my lamp burning;

my God turns my darkness to light.

The Lord lives! Praise be to my Rock!

Exalted be God my Savior! Therefore I will

praise you among the nations,

O Lord; I will sing praises to your name.

(PSALM 18:28, 46, 49, NIV)

CHAPTER ONE

WHERE ARE YOU?

(GENESIS 3:9, NIV)

Let the sweet wound of music enter your breast,
and let it speak to your heart.
It will drive out darkness and spread spiritual light
to every part of you.

—HILDEGARD OF BINGEN

O LIFE-GREEN FINGER OF GOD

O life-green finger of God,

    in you God has placed a garden.

You reflect heaven's eminent radiance like a raised pillar.

You are glorious as you perform God's deeds.

O sublime mountains, which can never be made low

    by the discretion of God.

Yet still you stand at a distance, as if in exile,

    but there is no armed power which can tear you away.

You are glorious as you perform God's deeds.

Glory to the One, the Body,

    and to the Holy Spirit.

Glorious you are, as you perform God's deeds.

—HILDEGARD OF BINGEN

*O*ur childhood memories, if we are among the lucky ones, are naturally filled with warm recollections of vast arrays of crayons and coloring books, brightly colored pens and pencils; delicate watercolors, and even splashes of finger-paint. With these simple tools, we could quietly slip away the hours of a rainy afternoon in passionate pursuit of the figures inside our mind, so that we might begin to transcend to another world. In this way, we could create private adventures and test our wings to fly from the nest. These experiments in creativity were our first movements into our imagination.

Our picture-drawing abilities progressed even further at story time. This was the hour or so when we sat quietly as a beloved parent or teacher related every detail of a time-honored tale. We cultivated our ability to paint pictures in our mind's eye as we listened with rapt attention. The ability to launch ourselves into our imaginative mind was encouraged, and something we looked forward to.

My childhood was one such as this, and to my mind my mother possessed special storytelling abilities. As she artfully changed the tone of her voice, I would sit as close to her as I could, savoring every nuance that she captured of the characters' unique and colorful personalities. I would be frustrated by other readings of the same story, thinking no one could live up to her standard of performance. With her voice, she opened my imagination and created my emotional connection to the story. I can still hear the intonation of her voice as she read to me... and I can see the little girl sitting there, quietly gazing at the book's illustrations, falling into them with her mind and soul. This ability to paint pictures in my mind, images that not only touched my heart but also personally connected me to the story, was the invaluable gift my mother gave to me through story time.

For some of us, this was the way we first experienced the stories of the Bible, too. And these early impressions, so carefully drawn in childhood, stayed with us and colored the beliefs we carried into adulthood. Coupled with our experience of the love we received from our parents, our interpretation and understanding of the underlying tone of these stories greatly influenced how we grew up to see the world around us. In this way, a lasting impression of God was created.

This is not to sound ominous; some of our impressions from childhood are good and should be maintained. However, the possibility exists that some of those impressions might be weak, or even unworthy of us. Still others might be incomplete impressions of a vast and powerful creator of the cosmos and everything in it. We can all agree that there is always more to know, more to understand, and to "see" with the eyes of a maturing and deepening faith.

Even if we realize our need to develop our picture of God, we have lost the skills required to make any adjustments. Somewhere along the way, we let go of our ability to create pictures in our mind as we pray or read the scriptures.

As these early creative methods fall out of use, we may also find that our relationship to God has become more distant—a matter of giving mental assent to ideas without reconsidering them, or trudging through repeated rituals without mindfulness.

At some point, many of us decide to grow up and let go of imaginative travels of the mind in favor of a more intellectually based study, firmly planting our minds in the historical context of the scriptures. These contextual studies are definitely valuable and most certainly should be pursued. But why should we sacrifice the lens of our imagination? When were we told that creative pastimes became "too childish"? Frankly, it is the idea that we have outgrown them that inhibits our spiritual growth. It is our inability to imagine ourselves in relation to God that can cause us to become stale and drift in our faith.

I have realized over time that an important part of our spiritual formation needs to be an ongoing development of our ideas and images of God—shading them in and adding depth, if you will. Our ability to picture him in our mind's eye and re-develop our "coloring-in" abilities of our youth can help here. I have gradually learned that our prayer life benefits greatly by holding a picture of our Creator in our mind and imagining him reacting as he listens to us. As Gregory Boyd writes in *Seeing Is Believing,* his book about imaginative prayer: *We need to imagine truth and savor it... we need to see pictures of grace in our mind's eye...we need to engage imaginatively in the unconditional love of God; only then can we break our addiction to hiding.*[1]

DEVOTIONAL PRAYER

As we press into this bright but largely unknown territory waiting to be explored of imaginative journeys towards and into God, I hope you will allow me to direct your thoughts towards our purpose in prayer.

Dear Lord, as we approach the familiar stories in the scriptures,
help us to open ourselves to new insights and understanding.
Help us to listen for your voice and to be fearless in our questioning.
Guide us now as we re-examine these passages of scripture with
our inner eye of faith. Take us into your word and renew our spirit
of understanding as we encourage one another to live in
greater awareness of your love.

To begin reshaping our image of God, it is important that we start at beginning with our creation story. It is in this opening garden scene of Genesis, so beautifully crafted to capture the deepest desires of our hearts, that we form our most lasting impressions of our Creator.

Now the Lord had planted a garden in the east, in Eden; and there he put the man that he had formed. And the Lord God made all kinds of trees grow out of the ground—trees that were pleasing to the eye and good for food. In the middle of the garden were the tree of life and the tree of the knowledge of good and evil. A river watering the garden flowed from Eden; from there it was separated into four headwaters.... The Lord took man and put him in the Garden of Eden to work it and take care for it. And the Lord God commanded the man, "You are free to eat from any tree in the garden; but you must not eat from the tree of the knowledge of good and evil; for when you eat of it you will surely die."[2]

Let yourself travel deeply into this description of the original Eden. Close your eyes and allow yourself to really visualize the virgin beauty of this garden and God's intimacy with his creation of man. Allow your picture to pull at your heart and fully embrace your inner longing for a greater connection to our origins.

ART: *Paul Gauguin: Frauen and Schimmel, 1903.*

Oil on canvas, 28 ½ x 36 inches. Museum of Fine Arts, Boston

We will begin our first exploration of the use of paintings with Paul Gauguin's depiction of paradise in *Frauen und Schimmel*. Before we examine the painting together, take a moment to experience it for yourself. Make a list of words that drift through your mind as you explore the painting. I have found this to be an effective way of understanding your reaction to any work of art. Your intellectual, emotional, and even your physical response to a painting is the artistic experience that all artists seek to create in you. In other words, the artist is endeavoring to create a new way to touch your heart or help you notice something you might not have otherwise become aware of. Gauguin stated this idea when he wrote the following description about his paintings:

> [T]hey do not give direct expression
> to any idea, their only purpose
> is to stimulate the imagination—
> just as music does without the aid
> of ideas or pictures.[3]

To start us in the process, my list of words for this painting reads like this: *Idyllic—Peaceful—Lush—Innocence—Green—Cross—Distant—Wistful.* When I view this painting, I can feel the heart of Gauguin

trying to express his dream of paradise. He knows it is there but he is still viewing it from a distance. I can relate to his sense that this place of beauty and peace are somehow out of reach, and I begin to question what it is that I am still wistfully longing for in my life … what is the deep desire of my heart?

The list of words you create as you gaze at this painting might be very different. As you meditate and journal about your observation of the painting, try to let go of any thoughts of inexperience you might have. Remember, there are no right or wrong answers in art. The artist is simply trying to reach out to you, to cause you to *sense* something. It is in this way the artist communicates and touches your heart. We can experience kinship or fellowship with the artist and he, in turn, can help us learn something new about ourselves in the process.

Now that you have spent some time with this painting, reread the scripture describing the Garden and take note of your impressions of God as illustrated by the words. Your notes might be something like: *He is generous—The plan is simple yet beautiful—Life is abundant—Man and Woman lack nothing—They live daily in the presence of God.*

Paul Gauguin's fascination with the story

of Paradise, represented in *Frauen und Schimmel*, beautifully illustrates his lifelong quest to capture on canvas the perfect garden described in the opening passage of Genesis. He stimulates in us the feeling of a lovely dream as it fades from our memory and he touches that which is deeply personal in all of us... our deep longing for God.

If you have any doubt of his biblical intent, a brief exploration of his work will uncover such paintings as *The Yellow Christ* (1889) or *Nativity* (1896). As you spend time with Gauguin's art, you will unravel a rich vocabulary of religious symbols. The universal meanings of these symbols are regular thematic material for many of his paintings. These symbols, frequently used in his self-portraits, would aid him as he regularly cast himself in the role of the artist who lived as the "suffering servant" removed from society. (See Descant: Self-Portrait later in this chapter.)

His personal story, in brief, is one of a wanderer searching for perfect communion with unspoiled cultures; or rather, the primitive peoples who lived apart from modern civilization. For Gauguin, these people, and the beauty of their lifestyle, represented man in perfect harmony with nature. He seems to be saying, "This is the way God intended us." Because of this, he elected to live among different native cultures, half-spectator and half-participant, in a constant effort to capture the beauty of their innocence on canvas. With his paintings, Gauguin seems to lead us to the very doorway of Eden and encourage us to imagine a life before Man ate from the Tree of the Knowledge of Good and Evil. He wants us to consider what life was like when "[t]he man and his wife were both naked, and felt no shame" (Gen. 2:25). Gauguin is provocatively suggesting the possibility that this garden, a place of perfect communion with God, might still exist.

Tempted as we might be by our universal dreams of escape, we all realize that we are living in the aftermath of man's "fall from grace." Because our understanding of this beginning greatly affects the tone and color of our journey, we benefit from questioning our view of these early events in the garden. As we read further into Genesis, we find the story of our beginning narrowing down to just one day, and a now famous conversation between a serpent and a woman who later became known as Eve.

One day Satan came along, disguised as a serpent, and told the woman a story, filling her head with lies. And these lies played upon her restless desire to become like God. Knowing her weakness, Satan encouraged her to feed her suspicious nature, and in so doing caused her to doubt God's good intentions. The woman began to think that maybe God was holding back from them, and that instead of being generous and loving, she considered the possibility he might instead be malevolent in some way. And so, she decided to eat of the Tree of the Knowledge of Good and Evil, and she encouraged Adam to eat of it, also.

When they do this, they agree to eat (or believe) Satan's lies. It is their distrust of God's good intentions that leaves them suddenly feeling vulnerable in their nakedness. "Then the eyes of both of them were opened, and they realized they were naked... and they hid from the Lord God among the trees of the garden" (see Genesis 3:7–8). They had lost faith in their picture of God, and this lack of faith caused them to feel shame and hide from God.

Adam and Eve's feelings of shame, ultimately leading to hiding from God, give life to Satan's words of doubt, and set the spiritual genetics of the human race. This event was the beginning of our mutual darkness—darkness that lives on in us, leading us to our own loneliness and separation from God. And the fruit of these lies is our fear of rejection and inferiority. We become afraid, like Adam and Eve, to show our imperfections, our "nakedness," to those around us. And because we have lost our ability to understand his good intentions for our lives, and his unconditional love, we too hid from God.

We do this as a society as we become accustomed to Satan's way of thinking, and metaphorically consume his brand of spiritual food. We no longer have a taste for the fruit that comes from the Tree of Life, from God. Instead, the things we crave are the things that are opposite from God's ways. Worry, anxiety, and an unhealthy need for constant affirmation inhabit our daily thoughts. Time passes, and we become used to our self-centered ways. We still have our deep longing for God, but we have forgotten how to find our way back into his presence. It becomes easier to pretend the suffering of darkness is just not there, and so we look the other way when ugliness presents itself. We are trained by those around us to focus on all the positives in life and keep a smile on our face.

ut then something happens, and each of us, in our own time, is forced to see certain truths of this world. A sudden death of a friend, prolonged suffering of a family member, or even our everyday struggles to pay bills and raise a family can cause an unsettling shift in our thinking.

It is in our individual times of trial that we can, like Eve, doubt God's care. Try as we might, we realize we have lost our ability to feel God's presence. He becomes distant to us, and in our disbelieving state of mind we, like Eve, are tempted to believe Satan's story and doubt God's good intentions.

Open the door of your heart now, and reflect further into the passage of the Garden. Ask yourself if you have any hidden or unexpressed feelings about this story. With honesty, journal your thoughts and try to open your heart to a time of prayerful listening to what the Spirit might be telling you through this painting. What are you noticing in this passage from Genesis, perhaps for the first time?

For my part, I had always viewed this story in the light of Adam and Eve's disobedience of God's command, and his need, being a just God, to punish them. And certainly there were consequences to their actions, but notice carefully the tone of God's relationship with them. In the middle of all of their hiding, God seeks reconciliation:

But the Lord God called to man,
"Where are you?"[4]

What a tremendous shift occurred in my thinking when I fully heard these words. A complete recoloring of God's nature occurs when we fully realize that God did not separate himself from humankind because of our imperfections—we separate ourselves from him.

God knew what they had done, but instead of forcing them out of their hiding place, he gently *called* to them. And afterward God did not leave Adam and Eve to stumble around in darkness outside of the garden... he *supported* them. I am touched when I read on to find:

The Lord God made garments
of skin for Adam and his wife
and clothed them.[5]

So what does a "Paradise Lost" look like today? What does our loss of connection to God feel like when expressed in words of our day and time? Each of us, being uniquely created, will have our own very individualized version of our journey with God. What can we discuss, however, that is deeply universal? How can we bring this story, which haunts us like a lost dream, closer to our heart and clearer in our mind?

In our post-modern world, I believe we could all benefit from unpacking the word "lost." This, then, will be our first step in our journey to a better understanding of our connection with God.

Lost—not knowing our way; a general feeling of aimlessness; without purpose.

Separate—isolation and loneliness; not feeling at home with any person or place.

Empty—nothing to give, used up; tired of everything and a total loss of interest in life.

Longing—restless and discontent with one's situation; feeling like there is something missing.

These emotions, if you really think about them, are signs of our general distrust of God. And while they may not be listed among the seven deadly sins, if left concealed long enough, these feelings can eventually draw us into deeper emotional addictions as we strive to fill their hole with various idols. These are the things that eventually lead us to emptiness when we devote an unhealthy amount of our self-worth to them. The job promotion, the perfect Prince Charming,

the dreamlike vacation, children that define our happiness, or even the constant pursuit of our dream house can lead us away from a deepening faith in God. These are the pursuits towards a growing self–reliance that ultimately fails us.

Even though I had made all the appropriate intellectual assents to God by agreeing that he existed, was indeed the supreme God; and had "put on Christ" in an adult believer's baptism... these emotions were still setting the tone of my day. Sleepless nights, petty arguments, and just a general feeling of dissatisfaction still plagued me, and I was quickly moving towards bitterness and despair. It was only when I began to think of my spiritual life as a continuing practice, realizing that my moment of becoming a Christian was only the beginning of the journey and not the destination, that I made real steps towards understanding my need for transformation.

Anyone can suddenly find himself in the wilderness when dealing with even the normal transitions of life. The sound of an empty house after the children have gone; the sense of loss of value after being passed over at work; the isolation and loneliness of retirement; all of these life passages can cause us to suddenly feel lost to the love of God. It is our inability to trust in God's constant presence that causes us to drift from one thing to another like a ghost searching for a place to rest.

It is in these precise moments that we need to resist the temptation to blame God, and learn to lean into him instead. If we awaken our minds to the possibility of God seeking our communion with him, then these trials will become like stepping-stones on a path to resurrection and new life with God.

The sixteenth-century mystic John of the Cross aptly labels our feelings of abandonment as the "dark nights of the soul." He openly expresses these feelings as part of our shared spiritual journey when he writes:

> [E]ven after we come to believe…
> we act like the blind and the deaf
> much of the time… Apart from God
> your soul is empty, without even
> a flicker of the Holy Spirit in it.
> And even after you believe you will
> remain largely subject to this dark
> condition until the eyes of your inner
> man are healed and opened. For this
> purpose the Holy Spirit is sent to
> blaze light of truth into your soul.[6]

The key to finding our place with God is to reshape our impression of his character. And so, no matter where life may currently find you, imagine God seeking you and calling: "Where are you?"

Travel again into Gauguin's painting of paradise, and rest in its beauty. Close your eyes now, envision yourself there, and bring the idyllic garden to life by engaging your senses. Slowly meditate on these questions:

* *What are you hearing?*

* *What kind of weather can you imagine feeling against your skin?*

* *What is your emotional response to this image?*

* *What do these feelings reveal to you?*

* *Does the painting lead you to some kind of peaceful memory?*

* *Or does it fill you with a longing for a country yet unknown?*

Before continuing, record your thoughts and answers to these questions in your personal journal.

Take a moment to linger one last time on the painting, focusing your eyes on the Cross in the distance, and wondering at its presence in the garden.

Imagine the Cross as a personal symbol, and think about your place in relationship to it.

No matter where you are on your spiritual journey, I encourage you to hear this passage from Paul's letter to the Christians at Corinth as if spoken directly to you:

Therefore we do not lose heart.
Though outwardly we are wasting away,
yet inwardly we are being renewed
day by day. [W]e fix our eyes not on
what is seen, but what is unseen.
For what is seen is temporary, but what
is unseen is eternal.[7]

RECOMMENDED LISTENING:
"O viriditas digiti Dei" by Hildegard von Bingen

To capture the feeling of wistfulness I believe exists in the paintings of Paul Gauguin I recommend listening to "O viriditas digiti Dei" by Hildegard von Bingen, as performed by Agnethe Christensen. Hildegard von Bingen's music is full of longing and desire for the undiscovered country of the Divine, and while there are many who perform her works, I especially enjoy the instrumental backgrounds that accompany Agnethe Christensen's vocals.

Hildegard von Bingen: Ave Generosa

"O viriditas digiti Dei" sung by Agnethe Christensen

Scandinavian Classics, 2014

ART: *Paul Gauguin, Caricature Self-Portrait, 1889.*

Oil on wood, 31 $^{3}/_{16}$ x 20 $^{3}/_{16}$ inches.

Chester Dale Collection, National Gallery of Art, Washington D.C.

Image courtesy of the NGA Open Access.

DESCANT: *Self-Portrait*

Paul Gauguin's (1848–1903) *Caricature Self-Portrait* shares with us a unique window into the soul of the artist challenging the world's view of the arts. Although he is classified as a post-impressionist painter, in order to better understand how to read his highly personalized style, it is important to note that he is considered to be the transformative leader of a nineteenth-century movement of artists fascinated with more primitive folk arts. Their artistic endeavors, deriving from a blend of African, Japanese, and Native American influences, relied heavily on conveying internal feelings through the use of symbols. Like music, the art of Gauguin (and later others, such as Picasso) would delight in the pursuit of expressing the inexpressible. Animal totems, geometric designs, stark colors, and exaggerated or floating body parts populate his imagery. His paintings reveal a life-long fascination with reoccurring universal themes of religious symbols and the connection these could make to represent the artists as creator.

I am charmed here by Gauguin's use of the term *caricature* and his desire to exaggerate, or use his talent for self-mockery. This painting, originally intended to decorate a cupboard door in the dining room of an inn, has ironically defined Gauguin and influenced the generations of artist that followed him.

Gauguin places his head as the primary focal point in two contrasting color zones, and surrounds himself with the ubiquitous religious symbols of the halo, the apple, and the snake. In this way, Gauguin sarcastically shares with us his inner struggle and tensional pull between good and evil. He seems to question his own motives, and portrays himself as part sinner and part saint in pursuit of a balance between his good intentions and what is required for his creative process.

For our purposes, it can be thought provoking to realize the variety of ways through which people express their personal identity. Fashion, home décor, love songs, scrapbooking, and even our new enthusiasm for selfies all highlight our common obsession with how we are seen by those around us.

REFLECT & JOURNAL

Jesus taught his disciples using metaphors that painted word pictures of the Divine. Continue with the idea of self-portrait as you read John 10:1—18. What kind of picture is Jesus painting of himself when he states, "I am the good shepherd" (v.11)? If you like, journal a list of adjectives you associate with the image of a shepherd watching over his flock. Close your eyes and begin to mentally paint a personal picture of Jesus as the Good Shepherd. What do you see? How does this scene make you feel? Take note of the emotions this title evokes in you as you continue to journal.

For more paintings by Paul Gauguin, search WikiArt for:

❖ *Self-Portrait with the Yellow Christ (1890—1)*
❖ *Where Do We Come From? What Are We? Where Are We Going? (1897—8)*

CHAPTER TWO

HOW WILL THIS BE?

(LUKE 1:34, NIV)

Darkness cannot drive out darkness: only light can do that.

Hate cannot drive out hate: only love can do that.

—MARTIN LUTHER KING JR.

STEPPING IN THE LIGHT

Trying to walk in the steps of the Savior,

Upward, still upward, we follow our Guide;

When we shall see Him, "the King in His beauty,"

Happy, how happy, our place at His side!

How beautiful to walk in the steps of the Savior,

Stepping in the light, stepping in the light,

How beautiful to walk in the steps of the Savior,

Led in paths of light.

—ELIZA E. HEWITT (1890)

Just as we can suddenly recognize the darkness of this world during our various trials, our heart can also unexpectedly be awakened to God's light. In a moment, our heart can be quickened to the warmth of his loving nature by something as surprising as the softly spoken word of a sympathetic stranger, or the beauty of the intricate weavings of a spider's web illuminated by the sun. Because our experience of God is so highly personal, attempting to describe it risks an incompleteness that would inevitably cause someone to feel excluded. God's love, being so perfect and universal in its nature, is impossible to completely describe. But trying to grasp his magnificent nature and wrap our arms around his constant presence is the journey set before each of us as we progress through life.

For my part, even though I had made a public confession of faith in Jesus when I was a child, it was more recently that I experienced a deeper awareness of his loveliness. Before this could happen, I had to feel a certain need for God; a kind of tiredness that finally produced a cry of the heart that caused me to turn to God in prayer. Overburdened by feelings of guilt and always sensing I wasn't quite good enough to be called a child of God, I prayed that he might somehow grant me the privilege of being a special light in his kingdom. I really had no idea what this might involve or how great or small his call would be, but in his impeccable way God answered me. In retrospect, I can see his hand in a slow process of preparing me for what would seem to me like a sudden epiphany.

This awakening of my heart happened one Saturday afternoon as I was watching Igor Stravinsky's *The Rite of Spring*, of all things. I had the privilege of playing the music of this ballet in college, and I have also listened to it many times as one of my colleagues performed, but I had never experienced the full performance version including the dance. Viewing it as an audience member provided me with my life-changing insight.

The story of this ballet, in brief, is of a primitive Russian folk culture conducting their annual pagan ritual sacrifice of a young virgin. I had never really thought about this title or considered the true meaning of an event of this kind. The frantic dance of the terrified young girl surrounded by a mob of villagers was so convincing that I was filled with compassion for her. My mind then leaped to thoughts of her parents, and what a horrible sacrifice they were expected to make to appease their gods. And in a sudden flash of understanding, I was struck by the amazing nature of God's gift of

Jesus. I could see with new eyes God's generous nature in the sacrifice of his son. God does not ask for our children as an appeasement for his "jealous nature." Instead, God loves us so much, desires us so much, that he reaches out to us and sacrifices the best of himself. The attractiveness of this idea had never really occurred to me before, and like a thunderbolt, I fell passionately in love with God.

This deep connection, made through an artistic experience, set the stage for my creation of my God thru the Arts ministry. God came to me in a moment, and I felt a call to show his love to others in a way that would change me and become my anchor in the storms of life to come. Even though my experience of awakening seemed to occur all at once, I can now see that the setup for this explosion of light that filled my soul was actually a slow process. God's hand was carefully arranging all the elements of my story to create in me a perfect moment of surrender. My feelings of emptiness that resulted in my need to pray were both important parts of my preparation for my coming encounter with God. He answered my request to become a light in his kingdom by opening my eyes to a uniquely personal understanding of what the word light *means*. Like the slow burn of a fuse

that ultimately ignited my inner fire, all the years of my silent reservation were preparing my heart so that I would, in his perfect timing, crumble and fall, resisting his courtship no longer.

God in his artistry has crafted a story such as this for each of us. His story is universal and multi-layered, and yet when you finally see his grace it is quite simple. As we begin exploring another aspect of his love, listen once more to the Gospel writer John, who reaches out to us and symbolically describes Jesus when he writes:

In the beginning was the Word, and the Word was with God, and the Word was God. He was with God in the beginning. Through him all things were made; without him nothing was made that has been made. In him was life, and that life was the light of men. The light shines in the darkness, but the darkness has not understood it... The Word became flesh and made his dwelling among us. We have seen his glory, the glory of the One and Only, who came from the Father, full of grace and truth... No one has ever seen God, but God the One and Only, who is at the Father's side, has made him known. [8]

From this passage, it seems that we should begin again in our understanding of God by a closer examination of what is meant by the word *light*. A conversation about our unspoken understanding of the word is an exercise I regularly practice with my college students as I work my way through the history of music in the Middle Ages each semester. It is beneficial to our study of this time period because the ideas associated with light versus dark are very significant to our understanding of the church and the art and music it nurtured. Through these conversations with my students, my eyes have been opened to see the Middle Ages anew as a time period obsessed with symbolically capturing God's light within their art. Illuminated manuscripts, golden icons, and towering cathedrals decorated with stained glass windows all work to feature the idea of God's light shining through the stories of the Bible and the lives of saints. These artisans seem to innately understand the sacred truths expressed in light. They know almost instinctively that these truths attract the eye and transform the heart of an individual, without requiring complete intellectual understanding.

With these images, they attempt to point the worshipers of their time to God's beauty and love. And they continue to inspire our souls to soar upward towards God each time we step into their presence.

So what is it that we subconsciously feel and know about light? What are the literal and abstract meanings of this word? And how can our deeper awareness of this lead us to a closer imitation of Jesus? Just as we have described darkness as the symbolic expression of our doubt leading to our feelings of fear, shame, and unworthiness, we can also understand light as the perfect symbolic antithesis. Light reveals and uncovers; it illuminates and enlightens our mind. Light by its very nature removes darkness. Therefore, light does not give rise to fear and doubt that lead to despair. It is our understanding and experiencing of light that gives us the courage to trust and our confidence in knowing whose love we can hope. Light does not shine into our hearts to judge our imperfections; light, when allowed full exposure, nurtures and heals the wounds of the world's darkness.

This naturally leads us to ask: How can this be? How can we reach out and accept his light? How can we hope to understand, and hold it inside us until it transforms our hearts and shines through our lives? And why should we even attempt this journey, since we are all saved by grace? Plainly said: it is appropriate for us to view the knowledge of light as something to be desired and attained, as Jesus describes himself as such: *"I am the light of the world. Whoever follows me will never walk in darkness, but will have the light of life"* (see John 8:12, NIV). And so we find that it is Jesus who heals the wounds of darkness; Jesus who will be worthy of our imitation; Jesus who will light our way and give us the wisdom to eliminate our blindness towards God.

To attempt to create a complete picture of Jesus we must begin by recognizing the unique significance of looking deeply into his first announcement, known as the Annunciation. This part of his story so closely associated with his birth and the Nativity is actually celebrated in both the Roman and Greek Orthodox liturgical calendar on March 25 as *The Feast of the Annunciation.* These practices, mentioned in church documents as early as A.D. 496, annually tied Jesus' conception closely with the season of his death, burial and resurrection. Therefore it is traditional to include Mary's conversation with the angel Gabriel outside of the Christmas season.

Each of the Gospel writers has uniquely crafted their point of attack to provide a special dimension to God's story of reconciliation. It is magnificent to realize the scope of God's plan when you zero in on the opening passages of Luke. As the story unfolds we are reminded that just as a woman named Eve initiated man's predilection for darkness and separation from God, Mary reconciles the world to God by giving birth to Jesus. In this brief conversation, Mary says *yes* to the impossible and reminds us of our attraction to God's light.

Spending time with this opening encounter with the Divine will then become the first stepping-stone on our journey to finding Jesus as a "light shining in darkness."

DEVOTIONAL PRAYER

*Dear Lord, be with us now as we reflect with new eyes
on one of the most profound moments in your holy scriptures.
Help us to see in a personal way the sacred truths
of the Annunciation. Open our hearts to witness this
miraculous moment when Heaven came
down to earth and touched the life of this rather young
and inexperienced Hebrew girl. And through her story
let us understand as the apostle Paul expressed:*

"For God, who said, 'Let light shine out of darkness,'
made his light shine in our hearts to give us the light
of the knowledge of the glory of God in the face of Christ'
(2 Corinthians 4:6, NIV)."

HENRY OSSAWA TANNER:
Annunciation

As we consider Mary's encounter with the angel Gabriel with fresh eyes, we will take time to consider the *Annunciation,* painted by Henry Ossawa Tanner (1859–1937). At a time when African-American artists were not yet accepted by the American art world, Tanner was the first to be internationally recognized. The first African American to study at the Pennsylvania Academy of the Fine Arts in Philadelphia, and the first to have his work accepted by the prestigious Salon of Paris in 1896, Tanner felt the dual burden of uplifting his race and expressing his religious beliefs through his artistic vision. It is interesting to consider how someone who experienced the discouragements of America's closed society could fill this painting of Mary with such brilliance of hope and spiritual awakening.

Tanner's *Annunciation* is strikingly different from any other version of this scene because of his use of the bright colors of yellow and red. To our eye, these are the colors associated with traffic signals, and so we can't help but stop and yield to its presence. Rather than the usual tranquil depictions of Mary, represented as if she might have been fully anticipating the angel's arrival, this painting reveals Mary as if awakened unexpectedly from a deep sleep. The angel, the messenger of light, is imagined here as a dazzling radiance slicing through the air to capture our attention, pulling us in to listen closely to the announcement that follows:

> *In the sixth month, God sent the angel Gabriel to Nazareth, a town in Galilee, to a virgin pledged to be married to a man named Joseph, a descendant of David. The virgins name was Mary. The angel went to her and said, "Greetings, you who are highly favored! The Lord is with you."*[9]

ART: *Henry Ossawa Tanner, Annunciation, 1898.*

Oil on canvas, 57 x 71 ¼ inches.

Philadelphia Museum of Art.

Tanner portrays Mary with an expression that is a mixture of fear and wonder, and we sympathize with her. "*Mary was greatly troubled at his words and wondered what kind of greeting this might be*" (v.29). What is also surprising to see is how he shows us a Mary who does not look away or hide her eyes. Instead of the typical gesture of humility, she is represented here facing the mysterious news almost unflinchingly. Tanner is encouraging us, in this way, to awaken our desires for God. With this painting, he shares with us his unique vision of Mary as she boldly sets in place a pattern for us to imitate as we long to live for Christ.

It is interesting to consider the life and times of the artist. Henry Ossawa Tanner, whose father was a minister in the African Methodist Episcopal Church and whose mother was born into slavery and escaped by way of the Underground Railroad, undoubtedly brought these elements to the canvas as he worked. Born just before the Civil War and influenced by the religious movement called the Third Great Awakening, Tanner displays an emotional vocabulary in color that simultaneously attracts and repels us. His firsthand knowledge of tumultuous historical events can be seen in his understanding of the use of brilliant colors, which express all the passion

of revolution. This Annunciation, unlike any other, draws us into the intensity and fire of one girl's religious experience as it sets the stage for the dialogue to come:

> But the angel said to her, "Do not
> be afraid, Mary, you have found
> favor with God. You will be with
> child and give birth to a son, and
> you are to give him the name Jesus.
> He will be great and he will be
> called the Son of the most High."[9]

This simple scene has so many dimensions that it really can help us to use the rich vocabulary of painting to explore them one by one. It is helpful as our initial meditation on this scene to consider it from the artist's perspective. To paint this famous moment would be overwhelming to say the least, but the artist would have to begin by wondering about the environment and activities of Mary on that day. Imagine yourself before a blank canvas, asking yourself questions such as, "What would Mary have been wearing? Or, "I wonder what the room was like as the angel appeared?" Doing this, you begin to make the scene real and personal.

The longer you consider the scene in this way, the more you make Mary real and personal. As you bring Mary fully into your imaginative mind and wonder at the manner in which God came to her, Jesus becomes more human... and even more mysterious, divine and human combined. This was my first experience of the Annunciation, and one that led to the writing of my first book. Mary became real to me through this process, and as she became real, so did Jesus.

Since then I have realized that a yearly re-examination of Mary's role in the life of Jesus can lead me to even deeper devotional thoughts, and every time I approach her I find something new to guide me into a closer walk with Jesus. I am confident that Mary's part in Jesus' story will continue to enrich my life for years to come. She is an ever-transmuting role model for me, and as I pass through different phases of my life, I anticipate that Mary will evolve from mother into disciple, hero, sister, and perhaps in the end, all of these at once.

So why should we, as disciples of Christ, spend time reflecting on Mary? How can placing ourselves into this moment help us on our way towards our transformation in Christ? Doubters might say that she is just a girl, with only a handful of appearances in the story of Jesus, and question how this young woman's reaction to God's news can be of any benefit to our pursuit of Christ today. Caryll Houselander answers it best in *The Reed of God* when she writes: "The one thing she did and does is the one thing that we all have to do, namely, to bear Christ into the world." She guides us on our way because "she was not asked to do anything in herself, but to let something be done to her."[10]

To experience this painting on a deeper level, we will change our perspective from that of the artist to placing our imaginative mind into Mary's shoes as she hears God's call: "The Lord God will give him the throne of his father David, and he will reign over the house of Jacob forever, his kingdom will never end" (Luke 1:32b-33, NIV).

Notice all the details of Tanner's painting. It is night; Mary is young; she is sitting in a very simple room with minimal objects decorating it. As you let your eyes travel around the room, you see a small lamp and several earthenware jars hugging the corners of the room. Tanner seems to be purposefully pairing these empty vessels with a small flame to suggest, to our subconscious, the idea of Mary becoming the receptacle of God's creative light.

The primary tensional element of the Annunciation that Tanner uniquely captures for us is the explosive burst of light revealing itself from heaven. This then is the long-awaited promise fulfilled after many generations of silence. What suddenly bursts into her awareness has actually been greatly anticipated for years and every episode of family history has played its part in preparing her for this moment.

You can't help but sympathize with Mary as she feels the weight of her place in the story when she says, "How will this be... since I am a virgin?" And when she does, Mary expresses the doubt we all feel when we dramatically see and hear God's call in our lives.

How will this be, that I should give up the security of my family's approval? How can it be that I raise the money to support this new endeavor? How can I face the ridicule of my friends? How can I face the challenge set before me without crumbling under the pressure? As she expresses her uncertainty, Mary gives voice to all of our reservations and fears. She looks into the mystery and dares to ask for the answers to all of our questions. She shares our mutual humanity when she openly demonstrates our need to see things clearly. As Mary articulates her doubt, she teaches us how to lean into God and rest in his care. Listen to the angel and hear these words personally:

The Holy Spirit will come upon you, and the power of the
Most High will overshadow you. So the holy one to be born will be
called the Son of God... For nothing is impossible with God.[12]

So often we forget that we have access to the creator of all heaven and earth. We are so distracted by all the noise of our lives that we can easily lose awareness of the fact that God is there with us. We are often so fearful of upsetting those around us that it can be difficult to find our courage, and yet God calls us in surprising ways if we learn to listen. At times, he may even require us to lose our spirit of timidity.

We admire courage in others. We are even attracted to their ability to throw caution to the wind or stand out in the crowd; and yet we become so overly concerned with how others see us that we find it difficult to imagine ourselves in new ways. Our survival instincts kick in as we worry about our reputation and the things people say about us. We worry that there will be those who pull away from us as they question our judgment or think we are foolish. What if our friends and family leave us when we need them most? And so we try to not make any big changes, and we work to keep the status quo.

Even though God accepts us in our fearful state, to help us mature as Christians over time God leads us to transform our hearts so that we may accept him in love. God imagines us how we might be if we lived fully trusting in his care. He sees us completely as we are, with all of our weaknesses, and plants dreams into our hearts that lead us to become more vibrant and fully alive to produce fruit in his garden.

But when we are filled with restless longings, we tend to struggle in our shame and attempt to hide our feelings. If only we could recognize these desires as God's way of leading us to his light! God works with each of us in a myriad of quiet ways to gently fill the whole of our empty places with his creative love that in turn will produce light in his kingdom. Lynn Anderson explains it in *Talking Back to God*:

> *Paying attention to our hunger for God and launching into the adventure is the first big step toward pursuing God. When we recognize this hunger is a desire God has put in our hearts for himself, we begin to open ourselves to ways of encountering that have endured since the first days of creation.* [13]

Even if we acknowledge that our desires are God-given, we still find ourselves asking, "How will this be?"

Mary shows us how to courageously step into our moment. Like a bride, she gives herself fully to God as she accepts: "I am the Lord's servant… may it be to me as you have said" (v.38). And as we fully view her in her ascent, she inspires us to play our own part in the writing of Jesus' story. Listen as Isaiah eloquently uses the marriage relationship to describe our relationship to God:

I delight greatly in the Lord;
my soul rejoices in my God.
For he has clothed me with garments
of salvation and arrayed me in a robe
of righteousness, as a bridegroom
adorns his head like a priest, and
as a bride adorns herself with jewels. For
as the soil makes the sprout come up and
a garden causes seeds to grow,
so the sovereign Lord will make
righteousness and praise spring up
before all the nations. [14]

To fully trust and empty ourselves of all our fears we must, like Mary, accept God.

To let go of all of our need to see things clearly and our desire to control the outcome, we must realize the simplicity of the message. Yes, God so loved the world that he gave us his only son, but look closely at the elements of the angel's specific message. Awaken to the beauty of these simple words spoken to Mary.

Fear not…
You are highly favored…
The Lord is with you…

When you fully realize these words as the *intent* of the message, it will change you. And when you can hear these words spoken to Mary as the Annunciation of God's love to the world, it will fill your soul with light. As Mary courageously stepped out in faith, she shows us how we can grab hold of the knowledge of these words that echo down through eternity and reconcile us to the confidence of our faith in God's love. Seeing Mary as our guide, we are inspired to commit ourselves to trust in God's good intentions no matter what life may bring us. In giving our assent we surrender our unconditional obedience to God's plan.

As you consider this scene one last time, look closely at all the dramatic colors Henry Ossawa Tanner used to express Mary's awakening. Let the red of the blanket envelop you and hold you closely as you hear these words spoken to your heart:

"Fear not _____, you who are highly favored by God! The Lord is with you."

And hear yourself answer back, "I am the Lord's servant... may it be to me as you have said" (v.38).

RECOMMENDED LISTENING:
*Ave Maria by J.S. Bach and Gounod, and
Ave Maria, Virgo Serena by Josquin des Prez*

There are so many beautiful musical versions of the Ave Maria written across several hundred years of musical history that it is difficult to decide on a favorite. For now, I recommend *Ave Maria* by J.S. Bach and Gounod, for its haunting melody set against a flowing backdrop of sound. For those of you who might like to try something a little more unfamiliar, the transcendent voices of the motet *Ave Maria, Virgo Serena* by Josquin des Prez is worthwhile. As you listen imagine it sung in the beautiful chapel decorated with stained-glass windows filled with light.

ART: *Henry Ossawa Tanner, The Banjo Lesson, 1893.*

Oil on canvas, 49 x 35 ½ inches.

Hampton University Museum, Hampton, Virginia.

DESCANT: *Sitting On the Father's Lap*

Henry Ossawa Tanner, labeled by some as a visual mystic, masterfully captures the kind of intimacy we all crave as he creates a magical moment between a father and a son. *The Banjo Lesson*, thought to be his greatest masterpiece, uncharacteristically presented the African American male with dignity to a world dominated by prejudice. Grounded in the African Methodist Episcopal Church's religious heritage of social justice, Tanner thought of his paintings as an act of worship, attempting to uplift the viewer by illustrating those things that were common to our human experience, and creating a bridge between the racial divides of his day.

Because I was immersed in a study of Mary when I discovered this image, I began to think of how domestic scenes such as this might have played out daily between the boy Jesus and his parents Mary and Joseph. They, too, must have gathered him into their arms and carefully nurtured him. Thinking about their care and envisioning this kind of scene in your heart creates an intimacy with Mary and Joseph that you may not have considered before. Thinking of them in this way brings new meaning to the statement "and the child grew and became strong; he was filled with wisdom, and the grace of God was upon him" (Luke 2:40).

Tanner draws us in and touches our hearts with an experience that is universally appealing by using two sources of light that illuminate the scene with a warm glow. From the left, you can imagine the twilight falling and shining through a partially covered window. It fills the room, spotlighting the milk pitcher and bread on the table. It is as if he is symbolically saying that these sacred moments are the true bread of life... these moments are filled with the *Divine*.

Everyone needs a little help from time to time, a little personalized attention from someone who cares. It seems we never get old enough to stop our hunger for intimacy. We easily love those who give of themselves in this way. And so we carry an idea or mental picture of having a special someone who is watching over us, protecting us. Someone who knows how to give us the space to try new things, but never lets us out of their sight. They are always building our confidence while still testing our resolve; always pushing, never giving up, constant in their care. Try to harness these universal feelings as you explore this painting further.

From the right, we can imagine a fire casting light on the people's faces as they focus on their mutual occupation. Tanner's brush strokes are loose, drawing us into the feeling of the scene; they draw our gaze to the more clearly defined eye of the father. He is relaxed, patient, and totally attentive as he watches over the child's progress.

If I breathe in very deeply and draw on this scene... if I close my eyes... I can almost imagine myself there sitting on the Father's lap, as he holds me safely in his warm embrace. I am not hiding in him, even though there have been times when I have. No, this time I am focused on the task at hand and confidently exploring, going fearlessly forward knowing that God is near. I feel his presence, and I sense that he is nodding and saying, "Yes, that's right... good... keep going... just keep going."

Take a moment and thank God for his constant presence in your life. And as you do, fully realize his loving care and *rest* in it. There is no need for a litany of thankfulness, no list of prayer requests; not today. There will be another time for that. For now, just bathe in the thought of his care, and think "you anoint my head with oil; my cup overflows" and "I will dwell in the house of the Lord forever" (Psalm 23:5b, 6b). Continue here in his presence. He holds you near; that is all. It is enough.

REFLECT & JOURNAL

As we imagine God seeking us and sustaining us with his loving presence we begin to hear the words of Jesus in new ways. Read Matthew 5:14—6 as Jesus commissions his followers to imagine themselves as the light of the world. Reflect and journal about the many possible meanings of the word light, and prayerfully consider how you might become your own unique expression of God's light to the world around you.

For more paintings by Henri Ossawa Tanner,
search Wikimedia Commons for:

❖ *Christ and His Mother Studying the Scriptures (1909)*

CHAPTER THREE

WHY HAVE YOU TREATED US LIKE THIS?

(LUKE 2:48, NIV)

Who loves a garden loves a greenhouse too.

—WILLIAM COWPER
(1731—1800)

GOD MOVES IN MYSTERIOUS WAYS

God moves in mysterious ways,

His wonders to perform;

He plants his footsteps in the sea,

and rides upon the storm.

Ye fearful saints, fresh courage take,

The clouds ye so much dread

Are big with mercy, and shall break

in blessings on your head.

His purposes will ripen fast,

unfolding every hour;

The bud may have a bitter taste,

but sweet will be the flower.

—WILLIAM COWPER, 1774 (V.1, 3,4)

At first glance, the art we will use to explore the next step, Vermeer's painting *Woman Holding a Balance*, might seem unrelated to our journey toward seeing Jesus. It has nonetheless held an attraction for me, and has helped me understand an important phase of evolving my experience of God's presence in my life. Vermeer's style is one that frequently captures these kinds of quiet moments of domestic life, and we can surmise from this that they held special attraction for him. I am inspired by how he masterfully conveys something that resonates deeply with us in these little vignettes of private solitude. He draws us in and allows us to observe the unguarded thoughts of this young woman, delicately expressed in her face.

Cultivating our skill of close observation is indeed the work set before us, as we learn to use paintings in our prayer and meditation. Our first step towards spending time with any work of art is to open ourselves to the idea that it can speak to us in a deep, unconscious way. It attracts us and pulls us into the scene, encouraging us to linger and to wonder about the connection our heart might be making long before our intellectual mind has had time

to unravel the meaning. These are the kinds of experiences that help us unlock hidden feelings, which left unchallenged can become stumbling blocks on our journey. This is why paintings, poetry, music, theater and dance can all in their unique way create lasting catharsis for our soul.

For me, what began only as a faint impression of this painting grew over time into a clearly defined picture of four universal elements of our spiritual journey: Light; Seed; Silence; and Germination. For when by seeing the glory of God's light, he plants a seed of desire for good works in our soul, we must first be transformed into his likeness through his silent reshaping of our purpose. This gentle breaking away, or "germination" of our will, produces his spirit within us far beyond what we could hope or imagine. The apostle Paul hints at our transformation process when he writes, "But we have this treasure in jars of clay to show that this all-surpassing power is from God and not from us" (2 Corinthians 4:7, NIV).

Let us look at these four elements of a spiritual journey in a general way, and then in context of various pieces of art.

LIGHT

As exciting as our dreams and awakenings are, at some point things narrow down to how we live our daily lives. All our ideals of light illuminating darkness must give rise to our ultimate purpose: How does the knowledge of God's goodness change us? If we can say that we have seen and understood light as Jesus, what does it mean for us to *become* light? As Jesus himself directs us:

> *You are the light of the world. A city on a hill cannot be hidden.*
> *Neither do people light a lamp and put it under a bowl.*
> *Instead they put it on its stand, and it gives light to everyone*
> *in the house. In the same way, let your light shine before men, that*
> *they may see your good deeds and praise your Father in heaven.*[15]

Try as we might, our progress towards shining a light can seem at times very slow. The events of our lives just don't unfold as we had imagined when we were first stirred by God's gentle touch. In time our discouragement can lead us to questioning God's very presence in our lives. As we feel our prayers are going unanswered, they become infrequent and grow cold, and living a life that always trusts, always hopes, and always perseveres seems somehow out of our reach. During these seasons of waiting, our inner light can dim, and we wander in our own personal wilderness. Struggling with our doubts, we begin to realize that picturing and admiring the gift of Jesus is different from desiring to become like him in his obedient nature.

SEED

In these times of what we perceive as God's silence, it is important to remember that as in all new flowering of growth, there is an important unseen process required. A seed is planted and then nourished by the elements of soil, water, and sun, and in all these things God finds a purpose. Beautiful new life springs from a source so small, so insignificant to our human eye that if we were in control we would certainly cast it away (see Mark 4:20). This mystery can be witnessed, as the divine miracle of God's creation process occurs every year, generating rebirth all around us. These unseen seasonal rhythms of preparation reach their peak as they burst forth in spring, bringing a splendid array of color to our hungry eyes and filling our hearts with praise for God's perfect timing.

SILENCE

Living in a fast-paced society as we do, we are ever pressed by those around us to be ever doing and producing. In light of this, it can be difficult to accept our need for a gestation period. In these times of our perceived dryness, we need to hold on to the knowledge that God has planted his spirit in each of us so that it may work towards transforming our lives. Like the seed, the beauty of our Christ-likeness needs time to develop, and nourishment to grow into the purpose that God has made for us, and our feelings of emptiness are an important part of our journey. Before we can find the balance of our relationship with him so that we seek his will in all that we do, we will fall and scrape our knees, clinging to the hope of having our own way.

GERMINATION

In these times, it is more important than ever that we continue to press into the darkness of our souls by focusing our minds in prayer. If we open ourselves and trust that we can let go of the things we hold most dear, we can begin to allow our hearts to once again feel the warmth of God's light directing us onward. When we learn to lean in and listen closely for his direction, his Spirit will gently unfold us to reveal that which is pure and powerfully created in his image.

ART: *Johannes Vermeer, The Allegory of Faith, c. 1670—72.*

Oil on canvas, 45 x 35 inches.

Friedsam Collection, Metropolitan Museum of Art, New York.

JOHANNES VERMEER:
Allegory of Faith

Light: Dutch artist Johannes (Jan) Vermeer (1632–1675) shares with us a perfect picture of religious zeal in his *Allegory of Faith*. This painting is filled with rich details, spilling over with religious symbols that are carefully placed around the room to provide us with meaning. Our eyes immediately fall on the lavishly dressed young woman as she clasps her heart and leans forward, riveted in her devotion to the crucifix. Her arm is leaning on the corner of a table that is holding the word of God. In this way, Vermeer suggests to us that the knowledge of Jesus' sacrifice is her cornerstone. The larger than life painting of Jesus suffering on the cross behind her amplifies this message and invites us to join her in her devotion. Under her feet are the symbols of worldliness, temptation, sin, and death; she has conquered their hold on her through her dedication to the cross.

Seed: Let your eyes travel around the painting to notice all the rich details. Encourage your mind to slow down and ask questions. Everything in this painting is carefully crafted to hold meaning. The room Vermeer has chosen might be in any middle-class home of his day, and so he is encouraging his viewer to find pieces of themselves in the painting. He is visually asking us to think of our own relationship to these sacred symbols, and how they find themselves in our homes. Art historian Norbert Schneider describes the purpose of religious symbols to the Dutch masters:

> [T]he application of religious motifs to everyday situations was typical to their work. The purpose of this was to bring the faithful closer to Biblical matters and to make them experience such as something that closely affected their own lives.[16]

As you consider the painting's meaning, look closely and notice that Vermeer has oddly dangled a glass ball over the woman's head. This crystal ball, a symbol of knowledge and intellect, encourages us to look deeply into this sacred mystery of Christ's passion. Vermeer gently reminds us of the multiple layers to Jesus' story, and entices us to press into the unseen.

Silence: Vermeer's idea and personification of faith as a perfect devotion to Christ's suffering might cause us to turn our heads away. We might feel it fine for some rare individuals, but realistically be glad that we are all made perfect by God's grace. Because of the human horror of the Crucifixion, we might choose to celebrate the divine nature of his Resurrection instead. And certainly, the sunrise and victory of Sunday morning and the generous nature of God's forgiveness is our prize; but if we desire to progress as disciples of Christ, surely the keys to our development must be held by the Cross. Again, it is our human feelings of guilt and shame that cause us to turn our heads, and it is our willful need to control things that keeps us from understanding God's ways. God knows us better than we know ourselves, however, and over time he allows us to feel the emptiness in our lives so that we desire with our whole heart to pursue his will for our lives.

When I look at this painting, I can faintly hear the words of Elizabeth Clephane's beautiful hymn written in 1872, "Beneath the Cross of Jesus":

> *O safe and happy shelter,*
> *O refuge tried and sweet,*
> *O trysting place where heaven's love*
> *and heaven's justice meet!*
> *As to the holy patriarchs,*
> *That wondrous dream was giv'n.*
> *So seems my Savior's cross to me,*
> *A ladder up to heav'n.*

Germination: Instead of turning away, begin again and prayerfully reflect on Vermeer's *Allegory of Faith*. Use your imagination to connect this image to pictures you may carry in your heart of those people you hold in high regard. Who is it you admire for their Christian strength and wisdom? You may find it difficult to express Jesus' perfect loving nature in just one person, so make a list of your role models and assign one attribute to each of them.

Someone on your list may have the gift of hospitality. Spend time in a memory of fellowship with that person, and thank God for their friendship. Someone else may have been an important mentor or champion that encouraged you in some special way. Again, spend time in thankfulness for that individual. Think of all the people who carry for you a unique portion of the picture of Christ.

I particularly admire people who are gracious under fire, and I also stand amazed at those who are eloquent in their public prayers. These are the living testaments of the power of God's Spirit when it is allowed to live within us, and when you take the time to hold them within your heart, they can inspire you to rise higher. Thank God for each of these true hearts that have been a blessing in your life; they shine like beacons of light to guide your way.

ART: *Johannes Vermeer, Woman Holding a Balance, 1664.*

Oil on canvas, 15 ⅝ x 14 inches.

Widener Collection, National Gallery of Art, Washington, D.C.

JOHANNES VERMEER:
Woman Holding a Balance

Light: In contrast, turn now to Vermeer's *Woman Holding a Balance* and simply take pleasure in admiring all the beauty and mystery it holds. Like other artists of his day, Vermeer was fascinated with the theatrical effects of light, and he delights in the challenge of representing it as it shines through the window from the left.

Famous for his portrayal of domestic scenes that capture the subject's inner spirit, Vermeer is commonly thought to be depicting a young woman tempted by her vanity. With this painting Vermeer not only demonstrates his ability to capture all the subtle nuisances of color but also his keen observations of the tension we experience between the human and the Divine. The sacred tension of *Woman Holding a Balance* is alluded to by his placement of a painting of Christ behind her, as he weighs our souls in the balance.

In this way, Vermeer encourages us to imagine ourselves in quiet moments of reflection. The ordinary subjects of his paintings profoundly bring us in contact with the sacred nature of our everyday life.

Seed: This young woman, who looks to be pregnant, seems to be considering all the things she has treasured in her life. Notice how the light breaks through the curtain and gradually shines through the darkness to cast a glow on her face. This light encircles her like a halo to suggest that she is doing sacred work. Her eyes are downcast, deep in concentration. While her outer garment creates a rich, protective shell, she is not wearing any of the expensive pearls that are common to Vermeer's paintings. Instead, the table directly in front of her seems to have been cleared; all the lavish gems are pushed to one side. She is gradually making room for new occupations, as the unborn life inside her forms.

Silence: To connect this painting to a specific episode in the Bible— and indeed the life of Christ— is difficult. Nevertheless, when you consider the great silence or gap in Jesus' life story, the years of his life not found in the Bible, the idea of waiting and preparation speaks loudly. If we continue in thinking of Mary and her mission of bearing Christ into the world, we find only these few words in Luke:

> *When Joseph and Mary had done everything required by the Law of the Lord, they returned to Galilee to their own town in Nazareth. And the child grew and became strong; he was filled with wisdom, and the grace of God was upon him.*[17]

Naturally we are curious about these years, and we can only imagine what their daily lives might have been like. Still, what is valuable to notice here is that Mary and Joseph returned home and lived quietly for many years, during which time they were responsible for nurturing and bringing up the Son of God. The labor of their hearts goes unseen, and occurs in the background as they set the stage for the drama to come. It was their honor to watch over Jesus as he grew from a boy into a man.

Germination: Our stories of how God works within each of us to bring his light into the world may vary, but the common thread among them will be that God will do *whatever* is required for our growth. Held within this concept is the harsh reality that often the extraordinary nature of our first awakening turns to the ordinary regularity of our everyday. In our disappointment, it may feel like God has left us to struggle alone. If we perceive this as a silence, it can become difficult to continue with our original fervor. At times it can be hard to accept how God could be working for our spiritual formation.

When we question God's methods, we become without realizing it the judge of God. We weigh his actions in the balance and decide if he is living up to our standard. Learning to lose our ideas of how things should be and letting go of our need to control becomes an important part of our spiritual growth process. It is during these quiet times that we should consider the possibility that God may be stretching us with his silence.

Light: As we transition our focus from Mary to Jesus, we will consider the only story we have of him as a young boy, lingering in the temple. It is touching to think of him eager to discuss spiritual matters with the teachers in the synagogue. Since this account is included in immediate relation to the infant stories, we might assume it was Mary who remembered it as significant. The power to light our way is held within this episode as we hear Jesus' first recorded words.

The story begins as Mary and Joseph have taken Jesus at the tender age of twelve to Jerusalem for the Feast of the Passover. We read in Luke 2:41–52 that upon their way home, they discovered Jesus was not among any of their friends or relatives. And so they returned to Jerusalem, searching for him everywhere. "After three days they found him in the temple courts sitting among the teachers, listening to them and asking them questions" (v.46)

I can easily sympathize with how agitated his parents must have been while anxiously searching for him, and I have always felt Jesus to be rather thoughtless of others in his preoccupation with religious studies. However, recently I have taken this feeling even further to consider how much our own human experience with Jesus has in common with Mary and Joseph in their pursuit of the lost child. The tone and color of their words have resonated with my own experience, and I believe they can provide an important method of access for our daily relationship with Jesus. Listen to what Mary says when, after all her frantic searching, she finally finds him: "Why have you treated us like this? Your father and I have been anxiously searching for you" (v.48).

Can't you feel her total frustration in those words? They must have been worried that something terrible had happened to him. And so, when Mary finds him totally rapt and unconcerned for their peace of mind, she is justifiably hurt. But if we bring the scene closer and hear Mary as she expresses all our anxieties when we feel that we have lost God's favor, we can be refreshed by the spiritual food of this story.

DEVOTIONAL PRAYER

Dear Lord, time and time again we rush headlong into

our day and forget to ask you to bless our journey.

Suddenly we realize we have once again lost the stabilizing

force of your presence, and we are filled with anxiety.

Help us now to silence the noise of all our concerns.

Help us, as we stumble, to feel your presence and

to know your love. Remind us of a special memory of the

touch of your Spirit within us. Help us to hold on to the

warmth of your grace. Forgive us all our controlling ways,

and speak to our hearts so that we may understand

your will for our lives.

REFLECT & JOURNAL

Take a moment to journal about a

time when you felt God answered your

prayers in the past. Make a listing of

all your concerns, and begin to imagine

God's intervention to resolve your cur–

rent worries. Breathe deeply and allow

yourself to trust in God's perfect love.

Seed: After the excitement of my awakening, I was passionate in my endeavor to share my newfound vision of God, and so I decided to dedicate my time and resources to writing a book. It became a dream to bring the story of Jesus' birth to life through the appreciation of classic art and music. The idea of being an advocate for the arts along with a missionary for God seemed heaven-sent. Writing a book about Christmas, I felt, would be a special way I could use the gifts and talents with which I had been blessed, and I was eager to begin.

Throughout this creative process I felt a great closeness to God. Rising several hours before dawn each day, I eagerly basked in his presence. While I had heard others describe writing as an arduous chore, my experience was not grueling in any way. Instead, each day I enthusiastically plowed forward, excited to discover my next epiphany. The more time I spent with the selected art and music, the more insights I received, and at times the ideas and words flowed so quickly they seemed as if they were being poured into me from a Divine source. It was only my own physical limitation that at times kept me struggling to keep up. I was confident. God was with me, and I looked forward with great anticipation to what the future would hold for me.

Silence: I find it embarrassing now to confess, but I felt my time of writing so miraculous that it stood to reason God would quickly guide me to someone that would be vibrating with anticipation to publish my book. In the months and years that followed, I found it difficult to understand the silencing of his involvement in my little book project. I felt my intentions were so noble that I could not understand why he allowed me to suffer such a long period of rejection. And as I stubbornly waited for the letter that would reaffirm my efforts, my book sat closed up tight, gathering dust under a chair in my study. In time, my self-esteem fell flat and my prayers grew cold.

Adding to this, over these same couple of years, friends that I had treasured for their emotional support began to be shifted away from me, one by one. I was adult enough to realize they weren't leaving me specifically, but it was still devastating to live through such losses to my inner circle. A dear old gentleman friend, with whom I could talk about anything, suddenly died; our closest neighbors, the people with whom we had exchanged keys and trusted to always be there in a crisis, moved away; my boss, who had mentored me for eighteen years, retired and also moved away; and several stalwart students whom I had come to think of as friends were relocated out of the area because of job changes. All of these close friends had in one way or another been my champions. In a great variety of ways, they had given me important emotional support through the years, and I couldn't understand why God would allow for so many of them to be taken away from me all at once. As self-centered as this all may sound, I found myself asking God, "Why are you treating me like this? Don't you know how much I have been doing for you?"

Germination: I wish I could say that I quickly found my way through this period of feeling sorry for myself, but before I was able to turn it around I had to endure a lot of emotional pain. In the end, however, I realized a shift in my thinking was required before I was ready to face what was ahead. It was only when I discovered that instead of judging God for his seeming lack of involvement, I must hold fast to the knowledge of his love and trust in his process that I began to move forward again. Only then was I able to consider that my will may not be in line with God's will and as I did this, I felt my peace and confidence return.

In all of my grand endeavors to please him, I had forgotten to make Jesus the center of my life. I had drifted away from the splendid beauty I had beheld within the Cross, and I struggled to even picture Jesus in my mind. In all of the religious zeal of my plans, I had tried to sidestep the transformation process, and in so doing I had lost the only thing that mattered: the gift of God's Son.

ook again at Vermeer's *Woman Holding a Balance*, and consider the things you are trying to balance in your life. What are the things you hold most dear? Certainly there can be monetary sacrifices we all can make, but to my mind, treasure can also mean people we love or even long-held sacred beliefs. You might prize your home, or the city you live in, or even your family. All of these things are good in themselves and blessings from God, but all can also become an obstacle to our progress. I love how C.S. Lewis expresses it in *The Weight of Glory*:

> *These things—the beauty, the memory of our own past—are good images of what we really desire; but if they are mistaken for the thing itself they turn into dumb idols, breaking the hearts of their worshippers. For they are not the thing itself; they are only the scent of a flower we have not found, the echo of a tune we have not heard, news from a country we have never yet visited.*[18]

Is God in some way urging you to let go of or move aside these earthly treasures? Consider how in holding on to them, you may be preventing yourself from moving forward. What activities can you decide to let go of to clear a place for new growth? How can you see God's hand preparing you for this next phase of your journey? Learning to stay open and available to following the Master's lead is a mystery that gently unfolds within you. Developing a relationship with Jesus begins with understanding his first words and hearing them expressed to us personally. Imagine yourself in the painting as you allow yourself time for quiet reflection. Imagine that you stop and feel the warmth of God's light on your face. Feel yourself letting go of your need to control things. Trust... and as you do, lean in to listen for his voice, perhaps hearing Jesus for the very first time as he speaks to you: "Why were you searching for me? Didn't you know I had to be in my Father's house?"

If we believe that Christ is the light of the world and we are to become like him, shining that light into the world, we must realize that he will first and foremost be closely representing God's will in our lives. Jesus will not be directed by what we think is best; he will always remain faithful to what he sees as God's ultimate purposes for us. Accepting this, then, we must learn to look for him in his Father's house. And as we let go of our will and turn to see him as the perfect representation of God's love, we imagine him with arms outstretched, calling us to commune with him there.

I want to encourage you to see yourself as you open toward him, looking forward and not behind, and knowing the strength of his arms will be there to catch you when you fall; no longer fearing the unknown or grieving for the past, but instead reaching out to take hold of his hands.

For you did not receive a spirit that makes you a slave again to fear,

but you received the Spirit of sonship. And by him we cry,

"Abba, Father." The Spirit himself testifies with our spirit that

we are God's children… we ourselves, who have the firstfruits of the

Spirit, groan inwardly as we wait eagerly for our adoption as sons…[19]

"Lift Thine Eyes" from Elijah by Mendelssohn

o find music that accurately captures the feelings of perseverance and waiting on the Lord, I highly recommend experiencing the story of the Old Testament prophet Elijah as retold in Mendelssohn's great oratorio *Elijah*. There are so many wonderful moments in this work, but for our purpose here I will suggest #28: *Lift Thine Eyes* sung by a trio of angels to comfort Elijah in his darkest hour (see Psalm 121:1).

Mendelssohn: Elijah

Part 2: "Lift Thine Eyes to the Mountains"
Paul Daniel, Edinburgh Festival Chorus and
the Orchestra of the Age of Enlightenment, Decca 1997

For other paintings by Jan Vermeer, search Wikimedia Commons for:

❖ *The Milkmaid (c. 1660)*
❖ *Christ in the House of Martha and Mary (c. 1655)*

CULTIVATING OUR INTIMACY WITH JESUS

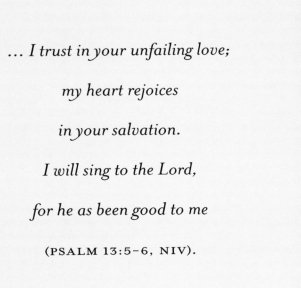

… I trust in your unfailing love;

my heart rejoices

in your salvation.

I will sing to the Lord,

for he as been good to me

(PSALM 13:5-6, NIV).

CHAPTER FOUR

WHAT KIND OF MAN IS THIS?

(MATTHEW 8:27)

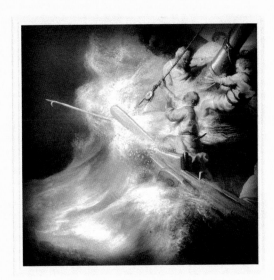

Simon Peter answered, "You are the Christ,
the Son of the living God."

—MATTHEW 16:16, NIV

LET THE LOWER LIGHTS BE BURNING

Brightly beams our Father's mercy

From His light house evermore,

But to us He gives the keeping

of the Lights along the shore.

Dark the night of sin has settled,

Loud the angry billows roar;

Eager eyes are watching, longing,

For the lights along the shore.

Trim your feeble lam, my brother!

Some poor sailor, tempest tossed.

Trying now to make the harbor,

In the darkness may be lost.

Let the lower lights be burning,

Send a gleam across the way!

Some poor fainting, struggling seaman

You may rescue, you may save.

—P. P. BLISS (1871)

We have pictured our ideal faith and committed ourselves to discerning God's will for our lives. Now, how can we deepen our view of Jesus, so that we may better see and know him?

Even though we might feel great affection for him, learning the art of our relationship to him can be disconnected from our daily life. How can we use the stories that comprise Jesus' ministry more effectively so that they may touch our hearts and transform our lives? As we are directed by the writer of Hebrews:

> Let us fix our eyes upon Jesus the author and perfecter of our faith, who for the joy set before him endured the cross, scorning its shame, and sat down at the right hand of the throne of God.[20]

Since Jesus has already written and achieved for us a full picture of God's love, we are called to gaze deeply into his mystery so that we may gain a greater personal knowledge of our part in his story. To help fit our lives with his likeness, we will next delve into individual scenes played out between Jesus and his disciples. As we linger over these precious moments, we will walk among his followers, feel their frustrations, and learn to listen for his words.

Where should we begin to witness the story of his adult ministry? Which episode would lead us most gracefully on our journey of picturing Jesus? Should we begin with one of the many miracles he performed, demonstrating the divine nature of his power? As we cast our eyes over the many episodes held within the pages of our Bible, perhaps we should consider one of his artfully crafted parables that tease our minds into considering our place in the Kingdom of God?

Very quickly, we realize that finding the perfect approach to Jesus, one that works for everyone in all phases of life, isn't really possible. Every one of us is at a different place in our relationship with him, and so we will each be drawn in by different parts of his story. The beauty and mystery of our life in him is that no matter where we are on our journey, Jesus can perfectly strengthen and feed us with his Spirit. We need only to quiet the noise of our busy lives and allow ourselves to linger, so that we may listen for his voice speaking to our heart. Developing our picture of Jesus is less about the perfect organization of his life events and more about allowing ourselves the time to step into his story, so we may better see and know him.

DEVOTIONAL PRAYER

Beautiful Jesus, Lamb of God who takes away

the sins of the world, help us as we long to bring

you into closer view. Guide our thoughts as we

consider this painting. Open our eyes so that we

may see you more clearly. Quiet the noise of our

lives, and help us to step into this scene so that we

may hear and see things more personally.

When you glance over the passages written about the early days of Jesus' ministry, you are left spinning at how quickly events are unfolding. Your mind whirls as you attempt to move with the disciples through each part of the story. His adult story begins as he goes into the desert to be baptized by John, and is then whisked away to be tempted by Satan for forty days. On his return to Nazareth, he is thrown out of the temple and narrowly escapes an angry mob, disappearing into the crowd. Then, walking by the Sea of Galilee, he begins calling his disciples. Soon after, they travel with him to celebrate a marriage feast in Cana, where they witness his first miracle of turning the water into wine.

After this, we witness one person after the other continually pressing him with requests. He heals the lame; returns sight to the blind; raises the dead; casts out demons, and finally at the peak of all this activity, we are allowed to pause on a mountainside to listen as he preaches the most radical sermon of all time, a sermon that turns everything upside down by teaching that the meek shall inherit the earth and the poor shall attain the kingdom of heaven. It is also remarkable in that Jesus does not elevate himself to the position of supreme ruler of mankind; instead, with simple words, he creates a vision of a new world order where those who follow him will be the "light of the world" shining the hope of peace so they, too, might be called "sons of God."

Because of his benevolent miracles and visionary thinking, it is not surprising that Jesus begins to draw huge crowds of people. As the word of his healing power spreads, more and more people press him for relief from their suffering, and we begin to feel the energy of a storm building around him.

It is amazing to consider that, in spite of the strain on him, Jesus never lost his desire to teach his disciples the principles of living in God's Kingdom. If we zoom in and listen, we can hear him say, "Others, like seed sown on good soil, hear the word, accept it, and produce a crop—thirty, sixty or even a hundred times what was sown" (Mark 4:20, NIV). Our hearts can easily understand the desire for productivity, and it is endearing to consider that Jesus might be expressing his dream for his handpicked inner circle of fishermen.

He knows, however, that the road ahead will be difficult for them. Knowing also that their time together is short, he ceaselessly guides them into a deeper understanding of the love of God. Feeling the tensional pull of the cross, Jesus understands that this unlikely band of brothers will be tested beyond their limits. He uniquely recognizes that before they can become the primary conduits of the gospel, they will need to learn how to trust in God's generous care. To do this, they need to learn that in times of doubt they must lean into his unseen presence and trust in his power to save them.

The disciples, on the other hand, are filled with youthful admiration for Jesus. Because of this they are eager to please him, and so they vie for his attention by asking questions. As they follow him from place to place, they are always listening and observing, but are still slow to understand the true meaning of Jesus' teachings. Constantly struggling to keep up with him, they attempt to direct and manage him. They have witnessed evidence to support a belief that Jesus is a man with special gifts, a teacher and a prophet; but they have yet to fully comprehend his divine nature as the Son of God.

Each time I immerse myself in these events, I marvel at Jesus' choice in selecting a group of unsuspecting fishermen as his inner circle. When I think of them traveling by foot around the countryside, I admire his willingness to work with each of them as they remained obstinately perplexed by the unfolding of Jesus' divine nature. He can see the content of their character and knows their potential to ignite the world. But Jesus also understands that to broaden and shift their focus so that they may become "fishers of men" (Mark 4:17), he will need to continue to open their inner eyes of faith.

You have to love the disciples, however, for their willingness to give up the security of their livelihood to follow Jesus into the unknown. Vincent van Gogh aptly characterizes the appealing nature of these fishermen when he writes:

The fishermen know that the sea is dangerous and the storm terrible, but they have never found these dangers sufficient reason for remaining a shore. [21]

And so, despite their inability to understand the true nature of Jesus, they follow him, hoping they will be rewarded in time. And things begin to happen to them.

When Jesus saw the crowd around him,
he gave orders to cross to the
other side of the lake…. "Follow me,
and let the dead bury the dead."
Then he got into the boat and his disciples
followed him. Without warning,
a furious storm came up on the lake,
so that the waves swept over the boat.
But Jesus was sleeping. The disciples
went and woke him, saying,
"Lord, save us! We're going to drown!"
He replied, "You of little faith,
why are you so afraid?" Then he got
up and rebuked the winds and the
waves, and it was completely calm.
The men were amazed and asked,
"What kind of man is this? Even the
winds and the waves obey him!" [22]

Did Jesus know there would be a storm? Was he using every event to teach his disciples? Most assuredly! He knows that in the days to come they will be tested to the limit of their abilities. The time will soon come when he will need them to be able to trust him enough, love him enough, that they will rise from the ashes of their grief and carry the story of his life into the rest of the world. And he issues a challenge:

If anyone would come after me, he must
deny himself, and take up his cross daily
and follow me. For whoever wants to
save his life will lose it, but whoever
loses his life for me will save it. [23]

When we see Jesus calming the storm, we witness an important moment for the disciples. Until now they have observed other people call out to him for healing. As they learn to face their own fears by calling on Jesus' power to save, they are readied for participation in his ministry. It is this moment when they let go of their desire to impress him, and truly make him their Lord.

In this way, the story of the storm perfectly encapsulates our journey as disciples of Christ. By spending focused time with these first disciples in crisis, we can find pieces of ourselves. As we allow ourselves to be pulled into the story, it cleanses our hearts and helps us let go of our need to control how we find Jesus in our lives. When we commit ourselves to the journey, we find that taking the next step means following Jesus into the storms of our lives and asking for his help as we cross over to the other side.

ART: *Rembrandt van Rijn, Christ in the Storm on the Lake of Galilee, 1633.*

Oil on canvas, 63 x 50.4 inches.

Currently stolen from Isabella Stewart Gardner Museum, Boston.

REMBRANDT VAN RIJN:
Christ in the Storm on the Lake of Galilee

To refresh and deepen our experience of this familiar story, we will deeply consider Rembrandt van Rijn (1606–69) and his *Christ in the Storm on the Lake of Galilee.* Known for his prolific output of religious paintings, Rembrandt has a keen eye and masterful hand at capturing the tension of the inner dialogue we can feel in a crisis. Lingering on the details of this painting, we can fully experience the universal nature of this story as it unfolds among Jesus' disciples.

To grab our attention and pull us into the painting, Rembrandt dramatically places a heavy mast that cuts a diagonal line through the picture, separating the light from the dark. Because of this, our eyes naturally gravitate to the more brightly lit area of the painting on the left. The storm rages, and the men balanced on the tip of a wave work with all their strength to fight against the strong wind. They attempt to pull the sail back in place and right the precarious craft that threatens to toss them into the sea. Despite their best efforts, the boat is still angled so dangerously upward that they are nearly overcome by the waves. Each of them is totally focused on their task of fighting against the power of the storm.

As you let your eyes travel around the painting, notice all the diagonal lines of the ropes that are holding the mast in place. One part of the rigging has snapped and flies haphazardly in the wind. Following this rope leads us to the darker side of the painting on the right. There in the stern of the ship we can see Jesus and his disciples awakening him. Notice how Jesus is pulling away as they surround him and try to press him into action. We can easily feel the tension of the previous moment when they forcefully shook him awake.

Continue to scan the scene. Try to internalize the expression that characterizes each individual, and notice how every element in the painting is carefully placed to express the most climatic moment in the story. As you carefully observe each member of this boating party, see how Rembrandt meticulously paints each gesture at the apex of its motion. Within the composition of this painting he assembles a group to fully reflect the complete range of human emotion as each man struggles against the storm. Like a well-choreographed dance, the movements within the group carefully highlight the different ways to react to a crisis. Some of the disciples are very active as they work hard to fight against the storm; others, unsure of their abilities, are paralyzed by their distress. We can pinpoint one man quietly praying, while another is violently heaving over the side. Within their range of emotions we observe struggle, perseverance, panic, resignation, stubborn denial, and raw fear. But despite the commotion that swept around him, Jesus... slept.

As a child, I was able to sleep deeply like this whenever I was on a car trip with my family. Being the baby of the family, it never occurred to me that I should worry while we were lost or experiencing bad weather. I had complete faith in the abilities of my parents and the intelligence of my older brother. Because I was confident of my safety in their care, I could always sleep peacefully, regardless of the pitch of their stress level.

So I can see here that Jesus is able to sleep because he places his complete trust in God, the powerful creator of all heaven and earth. He, too, is confident in his Father's love and knows that he is in his eternal care, despite the circumstances of the moment. He has meditated on the "splendor of the lilies" (Matthew 6:28) and has considered "God's eye is on the sparrow" (Matthew 10:29), and so, with the perfect faith of a child, he can sleep.

So how do we experience storms in our daily life? Certainly we have natural weather systems that remind us of the awe-inspiring power of nature. Recently, a terrible weather system threatened the safety of my family in Oklahoma for several days. The power and nature of the storm was severe enough to break off several miles of electric power poles, leaving them feeling vulnerable without power, cutting off their cable access to the outside world. There were others, however, who emerged from their hiding places to find that their houses were completely flattened around them. In these times, we realize that even though we may be able to better predict destructive storms, we are still left frightened by the tremendous force with which they can devastate our lives.

If we tap into the feelings storms can produce in us, we can use the story of Jesus calming the storm as an allegory of our soul. How can we look to Jesus when our world feels like it is spinning out of control? It helps, I believe, to prayerfully ask him to show us the root cause of our feelings of unrest. In this way we take time to wonder about why our emotions are tossing us to and fro.

When we deeply consider and simply express our feelings about life's storms, we usually realize that we are unsettled by our fear of something. Our "storms of doubt" arise within us as we fear losing something that gives us our sense of security.

For me, my greatest storm came when I felt called by God to seek a ministry in the greater Christian community. Over time I could see this meant I would leave the warmth of a church family within which I had formed deep-rooted emotional attachments. Because I had never really experienced any other way of worshipping on Sunday, going into the unknown was acutely terrifying for me. I could see that my vision for a greater involvement in God's Kingdom meant leaving my comfort zone, but the thought of hurting people I loved and possibly being misunderstood by them kept me from pursuing the dream God had placed in my heart.

Now as I look through the lens of this story, I can relate to the disciples battling against the storm. Because I have struggled with my own fears, I can imagine myself among them as they shook Jesus awake, and I can add my voice to theirs to say, "How can you expect me to leave the friends I hold so dear? How can I go someplace where I don't know anyone on Sunday morning? What if I unknowingly do something that offends someone? Or worse still, what if by leaving my church family and worshipping differently I offend God?" And as my excuses mounted, the tension of a storm grew inside me, until I found myself made so emotionally unhealthy from my resistance to God that I became physically sick. It was only when I finally realized that my security was in Jesus, who loved me so much that he sacrificed his life for mine on the Cross, that I began to feel calm.

As we experience the disciples in crisis, what can we express here that is universally manifested in our daily lives?

To do this we must put ourselves in their shoes and try to imagine their feelings before, during, and after the storm, thereby processing the story as if we were among them. We learn to hear Jesus' actions and words as if they are spoken to us in real time and personally. The more we do this, the more the lessons Jesus taught and the miracles he performed can transform our lives.

But what do we really know about these men? Being fishermen, the disciples must have had confidence in their own abilities to handle a boat in a variety of situations. When Jesus asked them to sail with him to the other side they must have jumped at the chance to care for him, and even show off their expertise a little bit. So when they were suddenly threatened by powerful waves, of course it was devastating to them. After all, their ability to sail a ship had been an important element of how they lived their lives and found their security. We could even say it was the source of their identity. Certainly we can see that they fought against the storm to save their lives, but they were also fighting to maintain the stability of something they loved—something that was their source of security and pride.

Like the disciples, we can feel unrest when the things we hold most dear are threatened. Our friends and family, our careers, our health, even being able to maintain a certain lifestyle or live in a particular neighborhood can unknowingly provide us with our sense of self. These things can provide us with symbols of what we perceive as our place in, and value to, the world. When sudden changes occur in our life's landscape, our fear of loss can cause us to rush here and there, thinking, as the disciples do, "Teacher, don't you care if we drown?" (Mark 4:38, NIV).

So what kind of man is this Jesus, who can sleep through a crisis and calm a storm?

If we pull back from the individual emotions and consider the overall meaning of Rembrandt's painting, we see the possibility of an even deeper message. If we count the figures we realize there are more than the traditional twelve disciples on this ship, which then leads us to ask who is the extra man sailing in their company?

The only figure we recognize for sure is Jesus; but notice then the man in the center of the boat, holding his cap on and looking out to sea. Rembrandt, familiar to us because of the multiple self-portraits he painted during his life, has carefully placed *himself* in the middle of the scene. If we follow the line of the rope he is leaning on, our eye is directed upward, pointing us to reconsider the huge mast, urging us to unravel the assumptions of our thinking; and now we see the mast looks strikingly like the Cross.

Thus we unconsciously begin to feel the tension of the future tragedy, when another group of men will use ropes to leverage a different stabilizing force into place. Rembrandt reminds us of the road to the Cross and hints at the fact that we are the ones who place Jesus there. Even so, he guides us into a suggestion that it will be our devotion to the Cross that will bring us through our personal storms of doubt.

Psychology professor Richard Beck, author of *The Slavery of Death*, describes the confidence we find in our devotion to the cross when we deeply understand that Christ's sacrifice frees us from the power our fear has over us:

Fearing death we act in a various ways that are prompted by our needs for self-preservations. [It is our] survival instincts that make us selfish, acquisitive, rivalrous and violent.

Beck continues to explain how Christ challenges this with his death on the cross:

Salvation in this view is obtained through Christ's defeat of the devil who uses our fear of death to hold us captive to sin, using our instinct for self-preservation to tempt us into sinful practices. [24]

Even if we are not consciously aware that our feelings of distress are caused by a fear of physical death, it is our unconscious anxieties about the death of our ego, our sense of self that can throw us into a state of crisis. In this way, fear is the most insidious and harmful of all our emotions, and with the story of Jesus calming the storm, he demonstrates his power to commandingly look into the face of fear and say, "Quiet! Be still!" (Mark 4:39).

Jesus knows us better than we know our-selves, and he understands how our fears can limit our lives. He understands how we often let our fears get the better of us, and so it is in such times that he wants us to call to him so that we may learn to lean into him for our security. Our faith grows as we learn to trust in him alone as our source of identity, confident in his love that will never fail.

Listen to those now famous words of Paul in his letter to the Romans:

Who shall separate us from the love of Christ? Shall trouble or hardship or persecution or famine or nakedness or danger or sword? ... No, in all these things we are more than conquerors through him who loved us. For I am convinced that neither death nor life, neither angels nor demons, neither the present nor the future, nor any powers, neither height nor depth nor anything else in all creation, will be able to separate us from the love of God that is in Christ Jesus our Lord.[25]

Return to the painting one last time and make it personal by stepping into the scene. As you visually complete each of their motions, allow yourself to engage your senses. Feel the unbalanced tilt of the boat as it is pressed by the storm. The wind and the rain are pelting your skin. Can you hear them as they shout directions to one another? Become involved with them in some way. Where are you in this scene in relation to the other disciples? Where are you in relation to Jesus? Take time to journal about your picture. What does this experience tell you about yourself? Can you think of a specific event or crisis that caused you to feel very unsettled and off balance? As you think about your own storm, hear these words personally:

Why are you so afraid?
Do you still have no faith? [26]

As your courage rises, trust in the nature of our Lord. What kind of man was he? Jesus is the Son of God, who has access to our supreme Father, creator of heaven and earth. We know him as the Divine, made human so that he may bring us into his kingdom to live "on earth as it is in heaven" (Matthew 6:10), and we trust in him who connects us to the power and the glory of his Holy Spirit, his spirit of peace that lives and reigns within us.

REFLECT & JOURNAL

As you reflect on these scriptures paired with the painting, think about a time when you felt your own "tempest of the soul." Continue by journaling about the kinds of things that usually cause you to lose sleep at night. What does it mean to "fix your eyes upon Jesus"? How can our view of the Cross provide us with our identity?

To look deeper and personalize another one of Jesus' miracles, read John 9:1—12 and consider how Jesus might be currently healing your own blindness. We all can admit that our daily business keeps us from fully seeing and hearing the Divine in our daily lives. What have your eyes most recently been opened to understanding more fully?

The Beatitudes by Arvo Pärt

My musical selection for this chapter is an exploration of the modern choral work *The Beatitudes* by Arvo Pärt (b. 1935). He is an Estonian composer of sacred music that will absolutely fill your heart with light. There are many wonderful recordings of this piece, but if pressed I would choose that by the English Chamber Orchestra, conducted by Nigel Short. They have many wonderful spiritual recordings in their catalog, but this work comes from a CD titled *Serenity: The Beauty of Arvo Pärt* (Decca, 2012). Arvo Pärt's music is very sparse, ideal for meditation, and this piece will guide you to a quiet inner place where you can focus deeply on the simple yet divine truths of Jesus' words as he speaks the Beatitudes, as recorded in the Gospel of Matthew. Allow yourself to imagine you are hearing them for the first time.

Serenity: The Beauty of Arvo Pärt

Track 7, "The Beatitudes"

Decca, 2012: Various artists

Rembrandt is one of the most prolific artists of the life of Christ.
To begin your exploration, look for these paintings in Wikimedia Commons:

❖ *The Supper at Emmaus (1629)*

❖ *Saint Paul at His Writing Desk (1630)*

ART: *Katsushika Hokusai, The Great Wave Off Kanagawa,*

first printed 1826–1833.

Color woodblock print from *Thirty-Six Views of Mount Fuji*

What are some practical steps to living more in the presence of Jesus every day? For this meditation I use a Japanese woodblock print called *The Great Wave off Kanagawa.* It is the first in a series of woodblock prints called *Thirty-Six Views of Mount Fuji* by Japanese artist Katsushika Hokusai (1760–1849). Since this is not a biblical scene, some might think it an odd choice; but if we are going to learn to live more in the presence of Jesus, we must start by broadening our definition of him. To do this, we must let go of our preconceptions of when and how we may find him. To live his abundant life, we must begin to allow him to show up in surprising ways. Living in his presence means opening our eyes as we are awakened from our blindness to see him all around us.

At first I thought it very odd for an artist to begin a series of prints about Mount Fuji with an image of a huge wave. I wondered what this artist might be trying to say to me. After a little digging, I discovered that to the Japanese people, Mount Fuji is the ultimate symbol of beauty. Because it is believed to hold the secrets of immortality, it has become a symbol of their cultural identity over time. Knowing this helped me to understand the deeper reasons for Hokusai's work; my heart recognizes a man dedicating the last years of his life to capturing the essence of this mountain. When you examine the entire series of prints, you can see his desire to connect the world with a beauty so great that it was like communing with perfection itself. He seems to be saying with these prints, *Slow down... look carefully at all the details... there is something very important here... appreciate the constant strength of the mountain's presence.*

Look again at Hokusai's *Great Wave,* and if you have not already discovered it, see that the wave actually frames the mountain in the distance. The wave is drawing our eye to the focal point of perfection, suggesting the way of a beautiful life. So perhaps what Hokusai is saying to us is that our identity, our beauty, and even our immortality, can be found in how we ride out these waves.

To bring this exotic scene closer to home, think of the some of the water imagery within the gospels. In one chapter Jesus calmed the storm; in another he walked on water; and still another we find him telling his disciples to cast their nets over the other side of the boat. These stories, recorded by his disciples, demonstrate the power of Jesus as we carry him with us into our lives. If, instead of focusing on the enormity of our battle, we trust in his strength to comfort us, we begin to let him gently guide our boat to safety through the storm.

But many times we are too busy and we forget to include him in our day. We become blind to his presence in our lives, and learning to keep our eyes fixed on him instead of the problem seems unnatural.

Realizing my blindness was the first step toward peace for me. I experienced my stress lifting as I gradually learned to invite Jesus into my boat. In this way, I was able to feel more lightness to my struggles. To trust Jesus with my life meant I had to first let go of the things that had given me a false security. My darkness lightened as I imagined myself letting go and trusting in God alone to handle my care. And as I did this, I heard Jesus speak to my heart: "Today you will be with me in Paradise" (Luke 23:43, NIV).

CHAPTER FIVE

LORD, DON'T YOU CARE?

(LUKE 10:40, NIV)

It is not enough to have a song on your lips.

You must also have a song in your heart.

—FANNY CROSBY

A WONDERFUL SAVIOR

A wonderful savior is Jesus my Lord, a wonderful Savior to me.

He hideth my soul in the cleft of the rock, where rivers of pleasure I see.

A wonderful Savior is Jesus my Lord,

He taketh my burden away; He holdeth me up and I shall not be moved,

He giveth me strength as my day.

With numberless blessings each moment He crowns;

and filled with His fullness divine,

I sing in my rapture, O glory to God for such a Redeemer as mine!

When clothed in His brightness, transported I rise to meet Him in clouds of the sky,

His perfect salvation, His wonderful love,

I'll shout with the Millions on high.

He hideth my soul in the cleft of the rock that shadows a dry, thirsty land.

He hideth my life in the depths of His love, and covers me there with His hand,

and covers me there with His hand.

—FANNY J. CROSBY (1890)

As we long for a closer relationship with a Savior, one that will comfort and guide us through the daily challenges of life, we must find a way of bringing Jesus into our everyday experience. We begin to realize the benefit of a more resilient and flexible view to find more intimacy with him. Our discipleship then becomes the desire to follow him and to move *with* him throughout our day. This means that as we attempt to understand a more complete picture of him, we need to change our vantage point several times.

Even when we believe in the power of Jesus to help us through our storms, losing ourselves to his care can feel impractical. We may realize our need to become more like him—we may even long for it with all our hearts—but something just keeps getting in the way of our intimate relationship with him. Learning the knack of a daily dependence on a Savior who cares for us individually can seem increasingly out of our reach.

This was my story as I savored my greater connection with God through the use of music and art. While my experience of the arts had warmed my heart and opened a doorway to a new revelation about the loving nature of God, Jesus still seemed elusive to me. I knew that if I wanted to live fully realizing the closeness of the words "what a friend we have in Jesus," there were still undiscovered depths to explore.

As I attempted to navigate life's challenges, Jesus' words came to me:

> *Come to me, all you who are weary and burdened, and I will give you rest. Take my yoke upon you and learn from me, for I am gentle and humble in heart, and you will find rest for your souls. For my yoke is easy and my burden is light.*[27]

But there was a time when this promise drifted farther from my reach and seeing the nature of an "easy and light" relationship with Jesus seemed as if I was looking through a cloudy glass. I could feel the warmth of his fellowship among certain individuals, but I couldn't find my private doorway to his affection. Despite my best efforts, I still felt I was the uninvited guest at the party, standing outside on the street, longing to be welcomed inside. For some reason still unknown to me, I couldn't manage to see Jesus clearly, and the God-shaped hole in my heart continued to go unfilled.

In time, I decided that some practical steps needed to be taken to deepen my prayer life so that I might be guided towards a clear understanding of him. *Maybe I skipped over some vital steps in the past*, I thought. For as much as I loved God the Father, to travel further in my spirituality meant I needed to discover my relationship with Jesus... perhaps for the first time.

DEVOTIONAL PRAYER

Oh how many times, dear Lord, have I come to these scriptures of comfort, and felt as if they were written about a flickering dream slipping from my grasp... a Garden of Eden for which the map has been lost.

Guide us as we learn to seek a greater knowledge of resting in your care. Help us to become awake to your presence each day, and when we do, help us to stop and really listen for the sound of your voice as you call us to reflect the light of your love into the world.

Desiring quality time to nurture our closeness with Jesus' unseen, divine nature challenges us, as our thoughts are often pulled between work, family, and friends. The ever-present temporal nature of our physical needs can naturally cause them to occupy higher priority with our time. Nevertheless, when we lose sight of Jesus and continually relinquish our spiritual work to "some other time," we find that our drifting can cause us some serious suffering.

Because my thoughts often wandered in prayer, I avoided calling on Jesus and let the urgent nature of my to-do list push me, rushing into my day. Days and weeks would go by before I even realized my need for prayer. In light of my neglect, it wasn't surprising that Jesus seemed distant and uninvolved in my life.

After a few disappointing attempts at a regular prayer time, I decided that if I was going to deepen my relationship with him, I needed more purpose and interaction with my prayer life. This ultimately meant finding a way to guide my thoughts so that I would learn to quiet my spirit and listen for his voice. If I desired to experience a relationship with Jesus so that his light would guide me through the dark times, I had to learn how to quiet my mind so that I might better hear his voice. The fourteenth-century mystic Julian of Norwich beautifully urges us to pray more in these times of busyness when she writes:

> *You may say your soul is too often tempted, troubled, and restless to pray, I tell you, that is exactly when you should pray… for the prayer of silence and waiting is the way to take hold of your unruly soul and keep it still until it is lovingly focused on God, made supple and ready to move again at His word of loving direction.* [28]

For me, being able to enter into "silence and waiting" required a vehicle to help channel my thoughts, so that I might find the time more insightful and the experience more interactive. I needed to learn how to ask thoughtful questions and quietly wait for God's answers. This meant finding something to do with my body while my mind was listening. A greater intimacy with Jesus developed when I learned to focus on him through a combination of Bible readings, meditating on music and paintings, and journaling. This injected a renewed freshness to familiar stories and allowed me to consider them from different perspectives.

I could slow down and ask questions that allowed me to wonder.

In this way, I allowed myself to listen and hear his voice. My feelings of being obligated or oppressed by prayer melted away, as I was able to perceive Jesus as approachable. Because of this, I found myself looking forward to my quiet time with him, and I began to find my prayer life more relevant to my day.

Throughout the ages, spiritual seekers have used a variety of things to help channel their thoughts. A candle, an icon, a poem, a piece of music, a hymn or praise song, or a scripture can all help rein in scattered thoughts and center the mind on the sacred nature of the divine. In this way, we allow ourselves to relax so that Jesus may have time to comfort and lead us. As we disengage and breathe in, he can remind us of our blessings and encourage us to open our eyes to new direction from him.

Paintings can help us center ourselves in our devotion and provide a focal point through which we can channel energy and learn to listen for insight. Juliet Benner, in her book *Contemplative Vision,* directs us in the practice of allowing paintings to "open us to new ways of seeing God" when she writes:

If we are seeking God, [paintings]
are not simply an aesthetic experience;
as we sit before them in prayer,
they become a means to open ourselves
to God... an aid to prayer. [29]

HENRYK SIEMIRADZKI:
Christ In the House of Martha and Mary

Learning to visualize Jesus by planting him into a realistic space can open our hearts to a greater emotional connection to a familiar passage of scripture. It can help us hear the story with our hearts so that we will be personally touched by his presence. Aided by the artist's creative mind, we can project ourselves into the scene to experience fresh insight into his nature.

ART: *Henryk Siemiradzki, Christ in the House of Martha and Mary, 1886.*

Oil on canvas, size unavailable.

Russian Museum, St. Petersburg, Russia.

I admire the artistry of Henryk Siemiradzki as he guides us with his vivid representation of Jesus resting at the home of Martha and Mary. The exotic nature of this scene is intriguing, and we take pleasure in viewing the various items he has carefully placed around the scene. The harp laying haphazardly against the wild rose vine... the repeating colorful pattern in the carpet... the open vessel... the birds casually flying in and feeding on the seeds... the grape vine... and Jesus himself, as he seems to gesture toward a tree. All of these things whisper the sacred themes of the gospels to the unconscious mind. When we allow ourselves to gaze at the story from the Bible through the lens of this beautiful painting, lingering to explore the subtle nuance of each detail, the story springs to life by engaging our senses. We are no longer reading about an event that happened two thousand years ago; instead, we experience the feelings of their encounter as if in the present. Jesus becomes more real to us, and we listen at his feet, like Mary. The idea of this can be so profoundly refreshing to our relationship with him that I want to encourage you to spend quality time in prayer with Siemiradzki's painting *Christ In the House of Martha and Mary*. I know you will find it an important step on your journey of seeing Jesus anew.

Since we now have experienced several paintings together, this time I will suggest the process as we move through the meditation of the painting. These steps, can easily, be repeated in various ways with any work of art. It is my hope they will give you the confidence to explore further on your own.

❖ *Begin by carefully reading the story:*

> *As Jesus and his disciples were on their way, he came to a village where a woman named Martha opened her home to him. She had a sister called Mary, who sat at the Lord's feet listening to what he said. But Martha was distracted by all the preparations that had to be made. She came to him and asked, "Lord, don't you care that my sister has left me to do the work by myself? Tell her to help me!" "Martha, Martha," the Lord answered, "you are worried and upset about many things, but only one thing is needed. Mary has chosen what is better, and it will not be taken away from her."* [30]

In your journal, make note of any thoughts you might have about this passage. Is there anything about it that has come into your awareness for the first time? Allow yourself to wonder about the personal nature of God's message for you.

❖ *Now, allow yourself to speculate about the personal message of the artist who illustrated this scene.*

With a little online research, something that can easily be done on your smartphone or tablet, you can uncover a few facts about the artist. Knowing the nature of the artist's surroundings can help you uncover a special connection to the painting. By imagining yourself in his place, you can begin to speculate about what might have been his motivation for choosing this specific subject, and in turn this can highlight the story in an unexpected way.

I will share with you the kind of storytelling you can create once you give yourself permission to wonder about the possible intention of the artist.

Polish artist Henryk Siemiradzki (1843–1902), a painter celebrated for his large religious canvases, moved to Rome in 1872 to surround himself with the countryside closer to classical antiquity. Because of his firsthand experience of the Greco-Roman world, he was able to create an atmosphere that was virtually photographic in detail and authenticity.

He brings this brief encounter between Jesus and Mary to life with his meticulous sculpting of light and shade. Notice how he captures the sunlight shining through the leaves of a tree. Though unseen, we can imagine the sumptuous branches of a large tree hanging overhead, providing ample shade for Jesus and Mary. Sadly, there are no specific dimensions available for this painting, and so we can only guess at its actual size. However, because it is listed with his other "monumental" paintings measuring as large as 11 ½ x 18 feet, we have reason to believe the size of this painting is impressive. You begin to realize the effect of its size when you think of yourself standing before a painting covering an entire wall of your living room. The artist entices us with an invitation to step into this idyllic scene by surrounding us with his larger-than-life vision.

As I cast my eyes around the painting to consider the specific varieties of the vegetation, I wonder about the connection this scenery might have to Siemiradzki's home. Because of the bright sunlit nature of the city of Rome paired with the monumental size of his paintings, I can imagine him working in a large space with huge windows opening to let the occasional breeze blow through the room. It was fashionable for artists to paint outdoors during his time, and so he might have wandered the countryside sketching different views of homes and various landscapes for his painting. Since many of the details of his life were submerged during the time of Soviet control, it is difficult to know the precise inspiration for the painting. However, we can postulate based on our knowledge of history and human nature.

❖ *View the painting again, thinking about the artist trying to speak to you from their own life experience.*

Over time, Siemiradzki's workshop became a tourist destination for those who admired his work. The idea of the artist opening his home to those wanting to view his paintings in the creative environment of the studio suggests a generous nature, and one that desired a connection with his viewers. It must have been a pleasure for him to witness their reactions as they appreciated the bright colors of his paintings. Their eagerness to stand before the product of his creative mind must have been a great source of encouragement that provided positive energy for further production.

This kind of active imagining about the artist working might seem surprising in light of the two-dimensional, fixed nature of a painting, but if you consider visual arts as a "performing art," an art form that requires an audience, the idea of the artist reaching out to you to share his heart can move you into becoming more actively involved with a painting.

Notice how Siemiradzki attracts and pulls us into the painting with a great wash of pastel blues and pinks. Trained as a scientist and mathematician, he demonstrates a special ability to bring a vast array of components together to achieve an effect. With his close attention to detail, he works his magic by surprising us with the idea of Jesus sitting on an enormous stone patio waiting to enjoy a common meal with his close friends Mary and Martha. Even though artists favored the practice of painting "plein air" or "open air" settings during the nineteenth century, we are still fascinated by the notion of Jesus stepping out of the dark alcoves of the cathedral into the warmth of bright sunlight. In this way, Siemiradzki's has created for us a new perceptive on Jesus. I am charmed by his desire to breathe new life into this story. I can see the openness of his heart and I am thrilled to see him throw open the doors of our churches to let Jesus roam the countryside.

❖ *Let yourself view the story from Martha's point of view:*

But Martha was distracted by all the preparations that had to be made.
(v.40)

Most of us can relate to Martha busily working to impress Jesus with her hospitality. Even if you have never considered the idea of hosting Jesus in your home, you can still identify with her desire to please her friends and loved ones with a flurry of activity. See her in your mind's eye as she is rushing here and there, fretting over all the preparations. Notice how preparing the food for Jesus and his companions is supremely important to her. Because of this, she becomes increasingly burdened by her feelings of frustration as she observes Jesus and Mary quietly talking, free from any physical or social concern.

Siemiradzki calculates Martha's feelings and astutely places her on the left side of the painting, standing in the shadows, viewing Mary's closeness to Jesus from a distance. We can clearly note her feelings of envy by the way she has crossed her arm over her body; our hearts understand her need for affirmation and fairness. With her body language, Martha is expressing the words already forming in her mind: "She came to him and asked, 'Lord, don't you care?'" [...] the Lord answered, "you are worried and upset about many things, but only one thing is needed" (v.40b, 41).

In her moment of questioning, Martha expresses our thoughts in those times we feel unnoticed by the world, overwhelmed by our daily tasks and under appreciated by those we love. Because we have become too busy to rest in the company of Jesus, we lose our connection to his Spirit. Not as a punishment for our neglect, for we know the unconditional nature of his love; no, it is our own fault that we stand apart in the shadows. We have lost or forgotten our knowledge of him, and so we begin to focus instead on keeping up appearances. As we mask our true identity with constant activity, we are the ones keeping ourselves from realizing the warmth of Jesus' care, and the self-important urgent nature of our lives leads us to forget our need to daily rest in his presence.

Burnt out, rejected, and disillusioned, in time we realize that none of our earthly endeavors can truly feed our spiritual needs. In the end, God works to lead us into a closer relationship with him despite our lack of understanding of his true nature. The apostle Paul echoes this when he writes:

> *Now to him who is able to do immeasurably more than all we ask or imagine, according to his power that is at work within us, to him be glory in the church and in Christ Jesus throughout all generations, for ever and ever! Amen.*[31]

In this way, I became so distracted by my need to be seen and appreciated that I began to form unhealthy attachments to find the affection I was missing. The thought that my actions might hurt the people I loved was pitted against resisting the tensional pull of my neediness, and created an intense emotional pain in me. I felt trapped, with no way out, and I wondered why God was allowing this to happen to me.

As I hovered near the brink of a fall, a wise and dear friend said to me: "Jennifer! Do you know how *precious* you are to God?" In retrospect, I believe she spoke these words over me very intentionally. The effect they had on me was like a mysterious incantation. I can still hear the sound of her voice calming my weary soul as her words unlocked the chains of bondage around me heart. No, I didn't realize the priceless nature of God's love for me; but as I allowed myself to grab hold of her vision, I began to imagine my relationship to Jesus differently.

Theologian Henri Nouwen openly writes about his feelings of despair:

> *I realized my increasing darkness, my feelings of rejection, my inordinate need for affection and affirmation, and my deep sense of not belonging were clear signs that I was not following the ways of God's spirit. The fruits of the spirit are not sadness, loneliness and separation, but joy, solitude, community and ministry* [32]

And this is how it is as we commune with our Lord. In spite of all our trying to see and know him, we realize our burden becomes lighter once we trust that Jesus is waiting for us to stop hiding and become more *real* for him. But first we need to lean into his unconditional love so that we can reveal our deepest thoughts, knowing he will never leave us.

❖ *Now take pleasure in seeing Mary sitting in stillness*
as she is listening and being close to Jesus.

In contrast to Martha's restless separation, Mary is content being close and listening as Jesus speaks to her alone. She is sitting unaware of the things that need to be done, captivated by his presence. Sitting at Jesus' feet, Mary's body language demonstrates to us how to be open and unconscious of time, like a child.

Consider this passage in Matthew and reflect on the characteristics of a child. Ask yourself, "What do I admire about children?"

I tell you the truth, unless you change and become like little children, you will never enter the kingdom of heaven. Therefore, whoever humbles himself like this child is the greatest in the kingdom of heaven. And whoever welcomes one such child in my name welcomes me.[33]

The thing we treasure most about children tends to be their innocence. Having complete faith in their parent's love for them, little ones are not burdened by doubt, and so are able to trust in their parent's intentions. A child's life in this regard can be carefree, giving them the ability to totally immerse themselves in play.

Children have not yet learned the appropriate social conventions, and because of this they are allowed to ask questions and to be curious. Free from fear of embarrassment, children have the ability to be painfully honest and open.

We could even say they are shameless when it comes to asking for something they single-mindedly desire. Still, these are the things we love and even admire about children.

When we see Mary sitting at Jesus' feet, we are viewing the perfection of a childlike faith. Mary is sitting close and relishing her time with Jesus. Letting go of her to-do list, she has stopped her activity and so she is free to open herself to him. Because she trusts in his care, she can lean in without concern of his disapproval or judgment. Her confidence in Jesus' love allows her to be curious and ask questions like a child.

Joanna Weaver, author of *Having a Mary Heart in a Martha World,* shares with us her experience of finding God when she writes:

> *...when I realized that holiness was a work of the spirit in my life, that my responsibility was to live connected to the vine, I was able to abandon my own fruitless trying and focus on staying close to the one who gives me life... Intimacy with God? It's pretty simple, really... It's not striving to know God, but realizing that our Father longs to know us.*[34]

What an amazing concept! I suddenly realized that perhaps I had the keys to feeling his love along. To think that I might have been blocking my own progress toward an intimate relationship with God! In all my years of Bible study in hopes of finding more information about Jesus, I had never stopped to consider that Jesus might be just as eagerly waiting for me to reveal myself to him. This idea caused a major shift in my thinking. The vision of my journey toward feeling this closeness to him was beginning to clarify.

And as I began to consider being more like a child, I thought, "Maybe the way for me to know Jesus better is for me to let him know me better. Maybe I shouldn't censor my conversation and thoughts by telling him only the things

I think are acceptable for him to hear. Maybe I should tell him everything... ask him for everything... even when I think his answer will be no."

As I became free and open, like a child, my relationship became more *real*. And even though I still felt myself resisting Jesus' presence, I found that he was able to hold me while I cried and kicked and screamed and fought against him. And as I continued to openly pray, I slowly felt him able to heal my broken spirit.

Take a moment now to think of something you might be a little ashamed of feeling. Look deeply into yourself and allow yourself to admit those things that hurt you. Tell Jesus your secret desires and share your pain with him. Tell him about the things you felt you deserved, or the people you might resent. Share with him all your feelings of loneliness and loss. Pour out your heart and become more honest about your state of mind. Instead of denying your emotions—, ask Jesus to show you their meaning.

Once you allow yourself to openly confess your thoughts, then turn and look up into his face. See there the look of tenderness in his eyes.

❖ *Return again to Siemiradzki's portrayal of Christ*
  In the House of Martha and Mary.

Continue to notice the type of trees and vegetation in the surroundings that give the picture all the vivid realism of light and shade. Can you connect the feeling of this place to anything you may have personally experienced before?

Become aware of all the details of Mary's apparel and the surrounding décor. Quiet the noise of your busy life so that your thirsty heart can drink in all the ambiance Siemiradzki creates by placing Jesus in a realistic landscape. As we do this, the story blooms in our mind and becomes alive to our senses. Jesus steps off the pages of the Gospel of Luke and becomes vibrantly real as Siemiradzki paints him resting on this particular hot and dusty day.

Observe how Jesus is tired, but confident and relaxed. Let your heart be touched by the sight of him spending time with one precious individual, and as you do this, breathe in the idea of Jesus being generous with his time. Really see him as he is, open to teaching anyone who comes to sit at his feet. While society might suggest otherwise, this young girl is worthy of his effort and his seeing: "Mary has chosen what is better, and it will not be taken away from her" (v.42b).

If you linger still longer, really immerse yourself in the scene and imagine all the sights and sounds that could possibly accompany the atmosphere. Can you feel the breeze as it blows through the trees, and hear the sounds of the birds singing sweetly overhead? Are there children playing in the distance?

Instead of keeping the scene at arm's length, why don't you step into it? Where would you choose to picture yourself in relation to Jesus? Are you an observer, or a participant in the conversation? Begin to visualize yourself being close to Jesus. Quiet your thoughts so that you can hear our Savior's voice. Imagine Jesus speaking to you personally. Allow yourself to explore the sound and cadence of his voice as you are still and listening. As you rest at Jesus' feet, what would he say to you?

At first, this kind of examination may seem a little uncomfortable, but when we dare to look closely and to linger in stillness, we might be surprised by what Jesus has to say to us. Listen now to Paul as he explains the work of the Spirit in us:

> [B]ecause those who are led by the Spirit of God are **sons** of God. For you did not receive a spirit that makes you a slave again to fear, but you received the Spirit of **sonship**.[35] [emphasis added]

Allowing myself time to sit at the feet of Jesus created a setting for me to hear his voice speaking to me personally. Allocating time in my day for a face-to-face meeting with Jesus produced in me a greater desire to hear God's direction for my life. I looked forward to my devotional time because I had opened my thoughts to his presence in my prayer and Bible study. As I did this, Jesus began to have more of a presence in my worship that continued with me throughout the week. Now, when I feel myself welling up to say, "Lord don't you care?" I am able to stop and hear him answer, "Yes, I care, and my love will not be taken away from you!"

REFLECT & JOURNAL

As we conclude our look at this episode in the life of Christ, imagine yourself in a private conversation with Jesus. See him as he is physically sitting in the room with you right now and ask yourself: What would we talk about? Resolve to take time each day to sit down and notice where you found Jesus in your day.

Joanna Weaver suggests:

Write Jesus a letter beginning with 'Lord, I know you love me because _____' and then list the ways he has shown his great love for you.[36]

For more paintings by Siemiradzki. search WikiArt for:

❖ *Christ and Sinner (The First Meeting of Christ & Mary Magdalene) (1873)*
❖ *Christ and the Samaritan Woman (1890)*

RECOMMENDED LISTENING:

"Come the Fount of Every Blessing"
sung by Lisa Arrington

For our meditation on freedom and divine grace, please consider the great Christian hymn "Come the Fount of Every Blessing" written in 1757 by English pastor Robert Robinson. The recording I recommend here is by Lisa Arrington, found on her CD *Farewell to Nauvoo*. The words remind us of the story in I Samuel 7:12, when the prophet Samuel raises a stone monument of Ebenezer to praise God's act of salvation. Ebenezer means "stone of hope," which in turn resonates with Martin Luther King's great "I Have a Dream" speech, when he says

*With this faith we will be able to hew out
of the mountain of despair a stone of hope.* [37]

Farewell to Nauvoo

Track 3, "Come the Fount of Every Blessing"

FiddleSticks, with Lisa Arrington, FiddleSticks 2004

ART: *Paul Landowski (designer),
Christ the Redeemer, 1922–31.*

Reinforced concrete and soapstone, 98 ft.

Corcovado, Rio de Janeiro, Brazil.

DESCANT: *Freedom in Christ*

It is for freedom that Christ has set us free... For in Christ Jesus...
[t]he only thing that counts is faith expressing itself in love. [38]

Seems simple enough—but how do we find ways to express our freedom in Christ? What does an open, accepting view of Jesus look like? Can you imagine the possible attraction for the world if we were to truly tap into this kind of an image of God?

Brazil is the largest country in South America and distinguishes itself with the colorful celebration of the pre-Lent Carnival season. The music that fills the streets during this time is a true sign of the flavor of these festivities, a unique mixture of the processionals, dances, and sacred dramas Portuguese missionaries brought to Brazil, paired with the syncopated rhythms of an earlier slave population showcased in the African drum ensembles. The indigenous people adopted these traditions and made them their own, demonstrating to us the heart of a people who are open to outsiders.

In light of this, think about the nature of the Christ the Redeemer statue perched high above the Brazilian city, Rio de Janiero

on the beautiful Corcovado Mountain. Built as a symbol of peace for a country separating church from state, it has become an important source of pride in their new identity.

Designed by French sculptor Paul Landowski in the new Art Deco style in vogue after the first World War, the statue was built by Brazilian engineer Heitor da Silva Costa, with assistance from French engineer Albert Caquot and the Romanian artist Gheorghe Leonida. Art Deco, with its emphasis on geometric shapes and clean straight-edged lines, was an exuberant and lavish celebration of the modern era. The style became a visual expression of optimism in modernity and a faith in social and technological progress of the time.

ART: *Christ the Redeemer*

statue on Corcovado Mountain

stands 98 feet tall on a 26-foot pedestal, his arms outstretched a grand 92 feet wide.

It is made of reinforced concrete and covered with thousands of soapstone mosaic tiles.

As I was writing this chapter about opening up to Jesus and seeing him in the open air, a friend of mine, Dr. John Hagemann, traveled to Rio and posted pictures of his experience of *Christ the Redeemer* online. I was touched by his bright smile as he stood in front of this impressive sculpture, as it seemed to perfectly express the open and accepting nature I have been attracted to when I visit his office.

When I asked him to explain more fully what surprised him about being in the presences of this magnificent statue, he described his breathtaking experience like this:

> *...what seems to be touching heaven,*
> *men and women of Brazil*
> *built this incredible statue of*
> *Jesus above the city.*[39]

It was not Dr. John's first visit to Rio, but more remarkable because:

> *This time the skies were beautiful.*
> *[So]many people, including myself,*
> *just looking up in amazement*
> *wondering how did they build this?*

He also describes the feeling of the statue as a constant presence as he toured the city:

> *... even more touching was seeing the*
> *Christ from the city. It seemed wherever*
> *you [went] in the different parts of the*
> *city, grabbing a glimpse of Corcovado*
> *brought a sense of familiarity of the*
> *icon that added to the excitement of*
> *being in this beautiful and proud city.*

It is wonderful to see how the collaboration of these artists continues to encourage the Brazilian people with their modern and forward-thinking vision of Jesus. Over time, it has become a symbol of the people of Rio de Janeiro that speaks of their open and accepting nature as they welcome each guest to their country.

Viewing this grand sculpture in partnership with Siemiradzki's painting of Mary sitting with Jesus in the open setting of an outdoor patio inspires my heart to sing as I realize anew what a wonderful savior we find in Jesus. It is my hope and prayer for you that you will continue to rest daily by his side.

CHAPTER SIX

DO YOU UNDERSTAND WHAT I HAVE DONE?

(JOHN 13: 12, NIV)

Once in an age God sends to some of us a friend who loves in us,
not a false-imagining, an unreal character,
but looking through the rubbish of our imperfections,
loves in us the divine ideal of our nature... loves,
not the man that we are, but the angel that we may be.

—HARRIET BEECHER STOWE

DOWN TO THE RIVER TO PRAY

As I went down to the river to pray studying about that good ol' way

and who shall wear the starry crown?

Good Lord show me the way!

O sisters, let's go down

Let's go down, come on down

O sisters, let's go down

Down in the river to pray

As I went down to the river to pray studying about that good ol' way

and who shall wear the starry crown?

Good Lord show me the way!

O brothers, let's go down

Let's go down, come on down

O brothers, let's go down

Down in the river to pray

—TRADITIONAL SPIRITUAL

*I*f we note how we most frequently see Jesus in our mind's eye, we might think of a picture of him on a well-worn prayer card that someone gave us as a child, or his image on a beautifully carved crucifix that adorns the altarpiece of a church sanctuary. Still others might think of the images evoked by a favorite hymn, or quote a particular passage of inspiration that holds personal meaning.

We all have personal and private ways of calling Jesus to mind, and so to replace old images with new ones might feel uncomfortable.

However, as we continue together in our quest of a more complete picture of Jesus, setting aside current impressions and exposing ourselves to new ones can open our hearts to a fresh flowering of growth in our imitation of Christ. To live as Christians who are full of love and free from care, we must be willing to develop our picture of Jesus.

Since God made his presence known to us in human form in a time before photography, we are not limited to a single visual in our understanding of him. Instead we are blessed with numerous descriptive titles of Jesus throughout the entire scope of the Bible. The Old Testament writers paint him as: a "sure foundation," the "rock of ages," (Isaiah 33:6, 26:4), our "Intercessor" in prayer (Job 16:20), and a "spring of living water" (Jeremiah 17:13). These comforting descriptions and many more culminate in Malachi with the news of "the messenger of the covenant, whom you desire, will come" (Malachi 3:1).

The writers of the New Testament are equally eloquent as they describe him as "the Lamb of God" (John 1:29), a "fragrant offering" (Ephesians 5:22), and "the bright morning star" (Revelations 22:16). And in particular Peter, whose name means rock, touchingly describes the very essence of Jesus as "the living stone" precious to God (1 Peter 2:4).

Each of these images deserves further reflection, but to take us even further in our devotion, notice the multifaceted way in which Jesus uses words to evoke imagery that speaks to our imaginative mind. Throughout his ministry he teaches us about himself with illustrative titles that seek to lead his followers into a greater connection with God. He is a source of our spiritual life as "the vine" (John 15:1), he is "the good shepherd" who cares for his sheep (John 10:11), and "the gate" leading us to salvation (John 10:8). He becomes our true love as the "bridegroom" (Luke 5:34–35), and then feeds us with his spiritual essence as the "true bread from heaven" (John 6:32). These images capture our hearts and fill us with wonder as we peel back the layers of their meaning.

As Jesus approaches a meal with his disciples, knowing it is their last supper together, he clings to these final precious moments. As he lingers on each face, he struggles for a way to create a lasting impression, a sort of "grand gesture" that will silence all their questioning and inspire them into greater maturity. A master teacher, he knows what is needed to capture their imagination and jolt them into a new way of thinking. Rather than continue in his preaching, he grabs their attention by doing something surprising and unprecedented. He strips off the outer layer of his clothes, kneels down, and begins to wash their feet.

Listen as John tells the story:

It was just before the Passover Feast. Jesus knew that the time had come for him to leave this world and go to the Father. Having loved his own who were in the world, he now showed them the full extent of his love. The evening meal was being served, and the devil had already prompted Judas Iscariot, son of Simon, to betray Jesus. Jesus knew that the Father had put all things under his power, and that he had come from God and was returning to God; so he got up from the meal, took off his outer clothing, and wrapped a towel around his waist. After that, he poured water in a basin and began to wash his disciples' feet, drying them with a towel that was wrapped around him.[40]

"Do you understand what I have done?"

With this question, Jesus signals us to stop and look closely. Can you see the importance of this gesture? How does viewing Jesus as he physically lowers himself to serve his disciples by washing their feet change our view of him? How can we approach this sacred moment with new eyes that transform our lives?

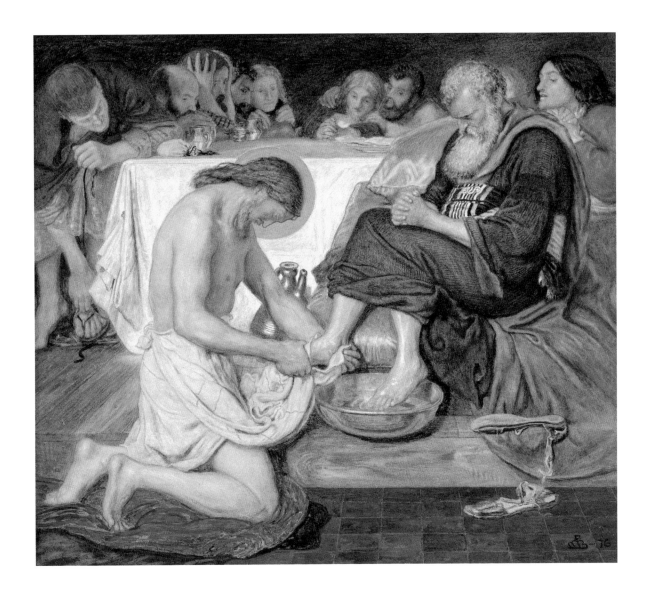

ART: *Ford Madox Brown, Jesus Washing Peter's Feet, 1876.*

Oil on canvas, 46 x 52 ½ inches.

Manchester Art Gallery, Manchester, UK.

FORD MADOX BROWN:
Jesus Washing Peter's Feet

Before we rush ahead to the transformational lessons of the Cross, we will pause and cleanse our hearts by exploring the painting *Jesus Washing Peter's Feet* by Ford Madox Brown (1821–93), and using it as a launch pad for our greater reflections.

Madox Brown was a British painter famous for his association with the Pre-Raphaelite brotherhood that included such artists as Gabriel Rossetti, John Everett Millais, and William Holman Hunt. Their style rejected the artistic trends of their day and longed for the purity and clean lines of the High Renaissance—in particular, the art of Raphael. With their use of vibrant colors and finely detailed realism, these artists were "committed to the idea of art's potential to change society," [41] says art historian Alison Smith, "by picking themes that told stories that challenged prevailing attitudes." This artistic brotherhood created a manifesto that clearly stated their views on art, and used a wide range of mediums other than painting that included stained glass, textiles, and furniture.

Madox Brown was fascinated with these artists, and while the bulk of his work is considered too modern for their typical literary subjects, his painting of Jesus washing the feet of Peter completely embraces and honors the ideals of their brotherhood by casting some of them in the story. (The model for Jesus was art critic F.G. Stephens, a well- known leader of the movement.) Madox Brown was also known for paintings that criticized the social fabric of English society and celebrated the workingman, as in his most celebrated painting *Work*. It is easy to see why this scene highlighting service and humility would appeal to him.

In studying the details of his life, I was charmed to learn of his association to the city of Manchester. I have lived and walked the streets of this great northern industrial city and so because of my time there I feel a special link to him. When I first learned of his historical murals in City Hall and how he opened a soup kitchen to feed the poverty-stricken people of his day, I resolved to return and visit these sights in the future. For now, I will fully appreciate the beauty of this moment of the Last Supper imagined through his eyes.

Madox Brown has composed this painting in such a way that it can work to stimulate the mind into greater thought. Instead of each element of the painting pulling you toward one focal point holding a unified meaning, this painting can be approached from multiple angles. We can view the disciples first as a group, and then individually as they each uniquely experience their encounter with Jesus. Paintings such as this can provide rich spiritual food, as they lead us deeper into the scene, allowing it to work as a fulcrum to shift our thoughts.

A lifetime of knowing this story, and yet I had not taken the time to linger with their different perspectives. As I fully considered each disciple's reaction to Jesus' simple yet profound action, it carried me beyond the painting and allowed me to tap into various personal memories that then led me back into a deeper connection with the painting; and in turn, the story; and ultimately—Jesus.

DEVOTIONAL PRAYER

Dear Heavenly Father, we pause and rest now, fully breathing

in the details of your last supper with your disciples.

Help us to realize more deeply the profound meaning of this

exchange between you and our brother Peter.

Because we are separated by time and space, we struggle with

our understanding of this tradition. Be with each of us,

guiding our hearts so that we may hear this story,

through the use of this painting, with a new and

personally cleansing message that will lighten our hearts

with a story of forgiveness.

Begin by noticing how Madox Brown presents Jesus from a unique viewing angle. From this lower perspective, we must mentally kneel to properly consider each disciple's reaction, played out in a very intimate compressed space. In this way, Madox Brown gives us a front-row seat to witness the unexpected nature of Jesus' action as he firmly holds and washes Peter's feet. As we experience this image it becomes like an icon that mysteriously sears our mind with a vision of humility. With this simple gesture, Jesus demonstrates his willingness to set aside his need for honor so that he might cleanse us of our self-centered ways. Our hearts are filled with admiration for a new kind of King—one who is tenderly serving us. With this act he gently signals the meaning of what will soon come to pass. As we look on with the disciples, we can place ourselves among them, preparing ourselves for the meal… and for God's mind-shattering display of love to come with Christ's death on the Cross.

Now rest your eyes on Peter and think of the conversation that will follow. His stern look suggests he might be humoring Jesus by letting him wash his feet, and most of us can sympathize with his look of discomfort. Madox Brown has portrayed Peter as an older man here; suggesting that the act of Jesus washing his feet might have been a memory that kept returning like the words of a familiar hymn coloring the passage of time. By painting him as an older man, Madox Brown is reminding us of the arc of Peter's journey, and the thought of how often the imperfect disciple was broken and yet always rose and began again, touches me.

Continue reading the story:

He came to Simon Peter, who said to him, "Lord, are you going to wash my feet?" Jesus replied, "You do not realize now what I am doing, but later you will understand." "No," said Peter, "you shall never wash my feet." Jesus answered, "Unless I wash you, you have no part with me." "Then Lord," Simon Peter replied, "not just my feet but my hands and my head as well!" Jesus answered, "A person who has had a bath needs only to wash his feet; his whole body is clean…." [42]

So many intimate moments between Jesus and Peter are conveyed through the scriptures that we naturally feel close to him as we wonder at his zealous personality. Peter is among the first to be called, and "at once they left their nets and followed" (Matthew 4:18); then he is the first to confess Jesus as "the Christ, the Son of the living God" (Matthew 16:15–16). Jesus then blesses him and gives him the "keys to the kingdom" (Matthew 16:19); but then in another version of the same story, Jesus also rebukes Peter for arguing with him about his death and says, "Get behind me Satan!" (Mark 8:32). In one chapter we read of Peter saying that he will die with Christ (Matthew 26:35), but then in the next few verses he denies he ever knew him (Matthew 26:72). He was then so grieved by his failure that he went away and "wept bitterly" (Luke 22:60–62).

As we read these stories of Peter, we notice something else about the man. Every time he fell he picked himself up and allowed himself to be cleansed by Jesus' forgiveness. Because of this, Jesus was able to refine this rough disciple into the bold leader who stood among the great crowd on the day of Pentecost and proclaimed Jesus as "Lord and Christ" (Acts 2:36).

In this way their relationship reminds me of a dance from Alvin Ailey's choreographic work *Revelations*, called "Fix Me Jesus." Through movement, this dance eloquently speaks of our lifelong spiritual growth as we allow Jesus to fix our brokenness. This intimate couple's dance creates a powerful image of our changing relationship with Jesus, as we experience it through a woman finding the balance of her faith and gradually leaning into her partner and his care.

In the beginning of the dance, Jesus shadows a young woman as she is navigates her daily life. With body language that mimics the idea of planting a seed that will bring a tender shoot of new growth, the young woman tenderly taps the air just above the ground and Jesus lovingly taps, too.

As the dance progresses the young woman experiences trials and storms; we see her swirling around the stage in confusion, moving in greater and greater circles away from Jesus. In time, however, she eventually finds her way back to him so that she may begin again. This time she stays close, fully trusting him and allowing herself to lean into the strength of his presence. He is there, supporting and guiding her body as she moves to the words, "Fix me, Jesus... fix me."

Their movements slow; she is tired, and life is nearly over. Then, as the lyric "fix me with my long white robe" is expressed, she begins to completely rest in his care. With one great swing of his arms they become one, and Jesus holds and lifts her high above his head. The dance finishes with the woman aloft, with her arms stretched out like a beautiful bird flying heavenwards. Seeing and experiencing this dance has become an important touchstone for my faith, providing me with a physical reminder that I must rest in Jesus' care.

Likewise, observing the honest way Madox Brown portrays Peter's relationship with Jesus helps me to feel and to know that this brokenness is a process that unfolds over a lifetime. I can see pieces of myself in Peter's reaction to Jesus here; I can hear my voice say, " No, you will never wash my feet!" Viewing the painting from this angle helps me to realize that as much as I love and adore Jesus, I can still resist his control in my life.

I am encouraged when I read Peter's expression of the arc of his journey: "Humble yourselves, therefore, under God's mighty hand, that he may lift you up in due time" (I Peter 5:6, NIV). And I can feel a type of brotherly love for him as I look once again to the painting.

While I still think about all this, I allow myself to consider the feelings of the entire group of disciples as they lean in and look on. Some are awestruck; others are horrified; and I think again:

"Do you understand what I have done?"

I naturally think about what it is like to teach and to be in front of a group of young people. Speaking in front of any group and looking into the faces of an audience can either give me an energetic lift or create a huge downdraft that causes me to struggle to find the right words. At times, it can be difficult to push against the resistance of their preconceived notions, and these well-worn grooves in their thinking can prove to be huge roadblocks to our progress. I confess that out of complete desperation I have often found myself being spontaneously and surprisingly silly in order to grab their attention to make a point.

Living in the time of the automobile, it is difficult to understand the symbolic nature of foot washing to the ancient civilization. As I drive my car from place to place and only walk as a means of exercise or recreation, the necessity of this ritual cleansing is obscure, and just seems eccentric to my mind, causing me to want to skip over further examination of the practice. But as Jesus has directed me to look carefully, I note my resistance and begin again.

Focusing on the ancient practice of foot washing, I am excited to discover the first reference of it in the Bible is found all the way back in a story about Abraham showing hospitality to his guests (Genesis 18:4.) I can begin to see this as a time-honored tradition, expected as the preparation for a special meal. Tradition dictated the person hosting the dinner would offer a little water and a servant to wash the dust from the travelers' feet before they would recline together around a common meal. It was seen as a custom of necessity, and a type of special welcome for a tired guest. In this instance, because they had come to a house that had been mysteriously reserved for them, the disciples seem to be unsure of what to do. When Jesus gets up from the table to take his place at their feet, he is clearly stating that he is the "host" of this meal, and with his actions we begin to understand the partaking of this meal is sharing in a new kind of hospitality from God.

As I look again to painting, I see the disciple on the left who is leaning in and untying his sandal. He is eagerly anticipating the moment when Jesus will wash his feet. While the others are still unsure they can allow this cleansing, this one is coming forward without hesitation.

"Do you understand what I have done?"

As I fully appreciate this disciple, I begin to think about being personally cleansed by Jesus. The idea of allowing myself to be renewed by his touch of grace so that his forgiveness can transform my life begins to powerfully move my heart towards Jesus. I can see with new eyes that we must first allow him to cleanse misconceptions from our hearts before we can humbly serve others. When we feel the mercy of his forgiveness we are freed from our guilt, and a new lightness is felt in our spirit. Fully realizing Jesus' consideration for our weakness allows us to have more compassion for others in their imperfections. We desire to humbly serve others when we confess our sins and allow Jesus to heal our wounds because we can feel a greater brotherhood with those around us.

I begin to feel myself in motion, no longer resisting Jesus' call, and as I am turning, I begin to hear deep down in my soul the call of the song "Down to the River to Pray". Originally an African-American slave song, it has become popular in recent years thanks to its appearance in the movie *O Brother, Where Art Thou?* The simple, repetitive nature of the words become meditative, and they fill my mind now with a vision of a slowly increasing crowd gathering at the river to be cleansed and renewed in their baptism.

As I went down to the river to pray
Studying about that good ol' way
And who shall wear the starry crown?
Good Lord, show me the way!

O sinners, let's go down
Let's go down, come on down
O sinners, let's go down
Down in the river to pray

Armed with this beautiful hymn, I return to the painting yet again. Now I can see and hear Jesus say to me, "Do you understand what I have done for you?" And I stand in silence, shaking my head as I answer, "No, Jesus, I really don't understand the fullness of your love."

Feeling my brokenness, I look at all the faces in the room and consider how the road to the Cross will personally challenge each of these men. One of them will betray Jesus; another will deny him; and all but one will abandon him. My heart melts at the sight of Jesus, kneeling there and reverently washing Peter's feet... and I am refreshed, to begin again.

When he had finished washing their feet, he put on his clothes and returned to his place. "Do you understand what I have done for you?" he asked them.

"You call me 'Teacher' and 'Lord' and rightly so, for that is what I am. Now that I, your Lord and Teacher, have washed your feet, you also should wash one another's feet. I have set you an example that you should do as I have done for you. I tell you the truth, no servant is greater than his master, nor is a messenger greater than the one who sent him. Now that you know these things you will be blessed if you do them." [43]

When I allowed myself to gaze deeply into the scene above, I realized that I have a Lord and King who has washed me, though I don't fully understand it. He is willing to kneel at my feet, and this thought opens and humbles me.

St. Francis of Assisi perfectly describes my feelings when he writes:

Deep within me the very wonder of it burns with holy fire... To have a God who has willingly and lovingly promised himself to us forever, so that He even calls himself our spouse! (see Jeremiah 3:14) And here is another great gift I carry within—A holy mystery, a wonderful thing that set me aflame with love... to have a Lord who calls himself our brother and our son! (see Mark 3:33—35). [44]

Now make it personal by imagining yourself among the disciples at the Last Supper. What does it feel like to watch Jesus wash their feet as you wait for your turn? Wonder about the feeling of Jesus holding and washing your feet. Imagine him touching you and tenderly cleansing you of all the dust from the roads you have traveled. Let go of your weariness and simply rest in his care as you join the growing chorus:

As I went down in the river to pray
Studying about that good ol' way
And who shall wear the star and crown?
Good Lord, show me the way...

REFLECT & JOURNAL

Read the description of the Suffering Servant in Isaiah 52:13—5, 53:1—12. Make a listing of all the different phrases he uses to describe the future Messiah of Israel. Close your eyes and allow yourself to form a picture of Jesus in your mind. Spend time in prayer journaling your thanksgiving and praise as you speak directly to Jesus.

ART : *Ford Madox Brown, Pretty Baa-Lambs, 1851–59.*

Oil on panel, 30 x 24 inches.

Birmingham Museum and Art Gallery, Birmingham, UK.

DESCANT : *The Lamb of God*

For our second course in this chapter we are celebrating all things British. This painting with its rich blues and idyllic English countryside is difficult to resist, and pairs perfectly with William Blake's poem *The Lamb*. I hope you will rest and meditate with these magnificent treasures, and then enjoy the recommended listening to deepen your experience.

For more paintings by Ford Madox Brown, search Wikimedia Commons for:

❖ *The Coat of Many Colours (1864–66)*   ❖ *The Ascension (date unknown)*

THE LAMB

Little Lamb, who made thee
Dost thou know who made thee,
Gave thee life and bid thee feed
By the stream and o'er the mead;
Gave thee clothing of delight,
Softest clothing, woolly, bright;
Gave thee such a tender voice,
Making all the vales rejoice?
Little Lamb, who made thee?
Dost thou know who made thee?

Little Lamb I'll tell thee;
Little Lamb I'll tell thee:
He is called by thy name,
For he calls himself a Lamb:
He is meek, and he is mild,
He became a little child.
I a child, and thou a lamb,
We are called by his name.
Little lamb, God bless thee!
Little lamb, God bless thee!

The Lamb by Sir John Taverner

*W*illiam Blake's classic poem *The Lamb* set to music by British composer Sir John Taverner gently guides us into a deeper awareness of God, and allows us to bathe in the glow of the moment. For this recording I recommend John Eliot Gardiner and the Monteverdi Choir on their CD *Christmas Adagios* (Decca, 2001).

Christmas Adagios

Disc 2, Track 11, "The Lamb" by John Taverner,

John Eliot Gardiner, Monteverdi Choir, Decca 2001

On the surface, Blake's poem is very simple and innocent, like a nursery rhyme. As you listen to Taverner's musical setting of this poem, it is interesting to hear how he begins with a dissonant and almost monotonous, trance-like melody to represent the discomfort of questions, of not knowing. He seems to be saying, "Do you know your creator? And how amazing he is?"

Notice how lovely it is when he has the choir slow down and lower their volume as he ramps up the harmonies. The music becomes all shimmering and warm as the questions are answered. He is letting us bathe in the glorious realization that God made the beauty of the lamb and the innocence of the child, and then he humbled himself to be called these things.

Listening to this, I can once again spend time drinking in an awareness of a God who is reaching out to me, treating me as his beloved child, and who is surprisingly different from anything I had imagined. Experiencing this fully leads me onward. Inspired by his great love for me, I realize I must travel further in redefining my relationship with Jesus. Confident now, I press on to stand at the foot of the Cross.

PART THREE

HEARING SIGNS
OF GRACE

You have made known

to me your path of life;

you will fill me with joy

in your presence,

with eternal pleasures

at your right hand

(PSALM 16: 11, NIV).

CHAPTER SEVEN
WHAT IS TRUTH?

(JOHN 18:38)

Everyone who is of the truth

hears my voice.

—JOHN 18:37B, NKJV

NONE OF SELF AND ALL OF THEE

Oh, the bitter pain and sorrow

That a time could ever be,

When I proudly said to Jesus,

"All of self, and none of Thee."

Yet He found me; I beheld Him

Bleeding on the accursed tree,

And my wistful heart said faintly,

"Some of self, and some of Thee."

Day by day His tender mercy,

Healing, helping, full and free,

Brought me lower while I whispered,

"Less of self, and more of Thee."

Higher than the highest heaven,

Deeper than the deepest sea,

Lord, Thy love at last has conquered:

"*None* of self, and *all* of Thee."

—THEODORE MONOD, 1875

Since the events most central to our Christian faith are those we celebrate during the seasons of Christmas and Easter, and because my first book focused on the Nativity, it has been a natural progression to think that I would eventually write a book focusing on Jesus' death on the Cross. While I have given several talks using the arts to guide my listeners into a greater experience of the Cross, it was overwhelming to consider spending extended time looking into this horror-filled event so that I might write a book. Still, it is my strong belief that standing firmly at the foot of the Cross is life-giving. And I pray that the experience of these meditations recorded here will be a source of light for all of us—perhaps especially for someone who may be struggling with a season of darkness.

Before we enter into this inner sanctuary of our faith, we should take a moment to examine why we resist looking deeply into Jesus' precious sacrifice. We might wear the Cross as a symbol of our faith, or sing about it in a song of worship, but we try to avoid letting our minds really linger over the details. Why?

The reasons I imagine are varied, and yet I am sure they are in many ways universal. Primary to our hesitation to view Jesus' suffering would be our human tendency to avoid thinking about death in any form, as it reminds us of the fragile nature of our own existence. Since we have trained ourselves (rightfully so) to get up every day and block the possibility of death reaching our door, the reminder of our mortality—in any format, whether it is in the evening news or our daily Bible study—challenges us and causes us discomfort. Because of this, we want to avoid thinking about suffering in any form, especially the suffering of our Lord and Savior.

Some may feel they have already heard the story, and so it is unnecessary to go through another recounting of the horrifying details. Others may have been taught with an over-emphasis of guilt, causing them to rush past the dark scenes of Jesus' death to the bright and joy-filled celebration of the empty tomb. But to do this requires some kind of special calisthenics in our thinking, doesn't it? After all, how can we celebrate his return to life when we haven't really experienced his death in the first place? In the end, all of us could admit to the fact that we busy ourselves with all kinds of distractions, so that we feel we don't have the time to look at Jesus' suffering on the Cross.

Whether it is for one or all of these reasons, so many of us become accustomed to our resistance to this part of Jesus' story. We still have our deep longing for God, but it becomes much easier to block our thoughts from Jesus' suffering, to look the other way, to focus on all the positives in our version of the gospel, and insist that we all keep a smile on our face.

But each of us will experience in some way the real ugliness in the world. Each of us will have an event that will change our view of things and cause us to question God. In everyone's life there will be a sudden death, or prolonged illness in the family, or a time of dealing with infidelities and addictions close to home. And we all despair, hearing about the continuing strife in the world and the constant news of terrible atrocities among us. For these reasons it becomes ever more difficult to hide our faces and pretend things will be all right. Try as we might to press our thoughts down and hide our wounds from each other, it becomes increasingly difficult to see the light because we have experienced the darkness so *personally*.

How do we combat the *whys* that crop up and take root in our thinking? And what do we tell people when they ask the age-old question of *Why do bad things happen to good people?* Do we have an answer that will calm their fears in these dark times? Or do we hear the voice inside our head whisper, *How can God be loving and allow such things to happen? Unthinkable!*

And so we quickly press this thought from our mind, and we wander even further away from ever knowing a deeper connection with Jesus.

Perhaps we should consider that this is where the Cross can be so powerful. Yes! Jesus died for our sins to give us the priceless gift of grace and the promise of heaven, but knowing this sometimes causes us to look away in shame that he needed to do that for us —for *me*. But maybe there is more to be seen at the foot of the Cross, if we really dare to look and listen. What if in Jesus' death he is showing us a new way to live? Surely, if I am to be crucified with Christ so that he might live through me, I must not be afraid to view his suffering... to really witness it until it refines and perfects me. (see Galatians 2:20-1, NIV)

Jim McGuiggan eloquently describes our need for looking deeply into the Cross in *The Dragon Slayer:*

It might make no sense because we don't understand the Cross. Maybe if we took a head-long dive into the meaning of the Cross and didn't come up for air until we are loaded with treasure... maybe we'll break the surface with eyes shining with excitement and broken hearts mysteriously healed. [45]

And McGuiggan hints at the life-giving wisdom to be discovered when he goes on to say:

As strange as it might sound, life begins with a long rapturous look at the death of Christ because if anyone has risen to fullness of life it is Jesus Christ and he did it through the Cross. So the Cross must be the way to life. His Cross must be the way to our life! And it is the way to life because in the end, the Cross is not about death at all.[46]

As a result, because I know there have been many artists and composers who have faithfully conveyed the message of the Cross, and because I believe that the greatest spiritual truths lie in paradox, I view Jesus' death knowing it is paramount to my own imitation of Christ. Standing resolute with eyes wide open, I have confidence that it will lead me towards my own resurrection.

JODIE MARIE ANNE RICHARDSON TRAUGOTT: *Crucifixion*

We will begin gradually cleansing our thoughts of various distractions by viewing an image created by a contemporary artist. This *Crucifixion* image was created by Jodie Marie Anne Richardson Traugott, or, as she signs her work, jm-ART. She is an artist who works in a "unique fusion" of mediums such as oil, acrylic, pastels, and here with her photography she uses what she refers to as her "contemporary digital magic."

145

ART: *Jodie Marie Anne Richardson Traugott (jm-ART), Crucifixion, 2013.*

Digital photograph, fineartamerican.com.[47]

While Ms. Traugott has an interest in a wide variety of subjects, she has always felt a special pull towards religious or sacred art. As I was able to communicate with Jodie several times, I was intrigued by her openness and ability to embrace her curiosity without the need to fit into some specific box. I became excited to find the heart of a kindred spirit when she wrote:

I never have preconceived ideas about where my art work is going as I'm creating it. It speaks, in a visual way, to me along the journey and tells me what it needs. It is only after something is finished that I find all kinds of personal meaning and symbology in it. But I try to allow the viewer to find their own! [48]

As she continues to describe her process, she tells that what began as a photograph of a crucifix taken at a "slightly odd angle" in a side chapel of the Cathedral Basilica of St. Francis in Santa Fe, New Mexico, turned into a fascination for her as the image became "progressively more interesting." Having a love for dramatic images with high contrast and intense saturated colors, she is attracted to sharp demarcations while working to combine geometric and organic shapes along with diagonal lines. Jodie writes:

I enjoy the process of crossing the boundaries from one discipline to another. […] This is a digitally altered/enhanced photo that has the look of a painting, drawing, etching, mosaic or stained glass. The "texture" is intentional and I feel it enhances the image and the illusion. [49]

Without completely understanding why my subconscious mind finds it so compelling, I feel fellowship with her as I gaze at her beautiful image of the Cross. Because of her artistry, I can begin to imagine the possibility of being simultaneously shocked and awe-inspired by being fully in the presence of Jesus' sacrifice on the Cross.

As I continued to look closely at Ms. Traugott's picture of the Cross, a list of words rose in my mind: *Mystery—Colors—Shifting/Changing—Dimensions—Voices.* These are the words that will begin our meditation of the Cross.

Mystery—Unknown or illusive meaning... meaning that is so profound that it is bottomless... meaning that is always feeding us with its presence without complete knowledge or understanding. As I view Jesus hanging on the Cross, I cannot imagine or understand the reason or need for his suffering. I cannot grasp or understand the pain he endured... I am humbled as I kneel before him.

Colors—Moods that turn, a complex pattern of thoughts and feelings in my mind. The variety of colors all need light to exist. Light, God's light, spotlights and highlights the beauty of the colors. To see and to understand, we must hold God's light within us... it is always present as our understanding turns.

Shifting/Changing—I see movement in this image; this leads me to think about new perspectives and changing ground. The odd angle helps me to see this image with new eyes and think about how we all change our view of the Cross throughout our lives.

Dimensions—Something about this image evokes the impression of time and space... the idea of infinity. I become more curious about the word *dimensions*. After some study, I learn that scientists have postulated there being as many as ten dimensions, leading to a limitless amount of possibilities in different versions of time. I think about how Jesus' blood was shed for us; how it is now cleansing our hearts; and has cleansed the hearts of those people who came in time before Christ, and

I am overwhelmed and humbled. Is Jesus still suffering? I wonder...

Voices—An event that is mysteriously colored by shifting dimensions producing multiple viewpoints and voices, all asking questions. What is truth? In the end, we can all hear an answer that will heal our individual wounds. Because of this, we gather at the Cross to silence all the voices of doubt, and to listen closely to our master's voice as he speaks these last words:

"I thirst." "My God why have you forsaken me?" "Father, forgive them for they know not...." "Woman, your son...." "Behold this day you will be with me in paradise." "Into your hands...." "It is finished."

God chose this dreadfully public spectacle to show his love for us, giving himself, becoming the perfect lamb who takes away the sins of the world. In so doing, he gives us his wonderful words of life. These words are Jesus' "tree of life." They give warmth and light to show us how to grow new life, how to find our way to our own personal resurrection (see Revelation 22:1–2).

As I linger over his last words, what begins to float to the surface of my reflections is a greater realization that in the last hours of Christ's suffering, he is living and dying, teaching the Sermon on the Mount. When we spend time here at the foot of the Cross, listening, we learn how to step into our own moment, and when we do this, we begin to understand how to commune at our Savior's side.

Yes, I believe in the profound importance of standing at the foot of the Cross, because this is where I have experienced true healing. Derek Flood writes of our need for a heartfelt personal experience of the Cross in *Healing the Gospel*:

> *We cannot truly understand something when we observe it "objectively" from a distance. We understand when it pounds in our chest, when it impacts us. We only truly know something when we are in the middle of it.... Spiritual things must be spoken of in the language of analogy and drama because they are so much beyond our words to capture, and because we need the passion that these images evoke to get hold of the depth and gravity of these ideas.* [50]

I hope you will resist the temptation to put the book down at this point.
Instead I invite you to join me. "Come let us go up to the mountain of the Lord,
to the house of the God of Jacob. He will teach us his ways
so that we may walk in his paths" (Isaiah 2:3, NIV).
Let us resolve to linger together as we learn to treasure these words
that Jesus spoke as he suffered on the Tree of *Life*.

MUSICAL MEDITATION:
The Seven Last Words

Rather than a straightforward narrative of the passion, these Seven Last Words (or phrases) of Christ on the Cross have been used traditionally as a vehicle for reflection during Good Friday services. The following order of these phrases is the one most commonly used, and comes from a compilation from all four Gospels.

As you listen to the following selections of music, I encourage you to close your eyes and allow yourself to be fully present in the moment. Let any images that may come arise in your mind. You should feel no pressure to do things in any particular order or for a certain amount of time. You may journal your thoughts, or begin to form a prayer; there are really no rules. Just let yourself be carried away into the scene of the passion of the Christ.

The Seven Last Words of Christ on the Cross (oratorio version), Joseph Haydn

Movement I: Introduction,

Nicol Matt, Chamber Choir of Europe,

Kurpfälzisches Kammerorchester Mannheim, Brilliant Classics 2012

DEVOTIONAL PRAYER

Dear Lord, as we continue our journey with you,

in this your way of the Cross, we must admit that we do not

understand the great mysteries—the great whys of this life.

We are burdened and perplexed by all that we must endure

in this world and we look to you now for your strength

and guidance. Dearest Jesus, we do not like to look upon your

suffering or think about our need for the shedding of

your blood. It gives us great discomfort to think of

your agony on the Cross. Help us now as we place ourselves at

the foot of the Cross to stand, firm in your presence.

FATHER, FORGIVE THEM, FOR THEY
DO NOT KNOW WHAT THEY ARE DOING

Think first about the all the humiliation Jesus experienced before and during his crucifixion. The soldiers verbally abused him and spat on him as they brutally beat him, hitting his face with their fists. They shamed him further by stripping him of his clothes, and mocked him by placing a robe around his shoulders, a stick for his scepter in his hand as they thrust a crown of thorns on his head. He becomes our man of sorrow (see Isaiah 53:3).

As they march him up the hill to his place of execution, he falls several times and so the soldiers force Simon of Cyrene to carry his Cross for him. Jesus is alone, in the middle of a sea of people who are taunting and hurling insults at him. He does not resist or try to defend himself in any way; there is no way out for him, the path is already chosen. The hands that healed the blind are now opened to accept the nails affixing him to the Cross. He is lifted up and into place... and we shudder at the horror of it.

Then we hear Jesus' voice as he struggles to speak:

"Father, forgive them, for they
do not know what they are doing." [51]

And so to hear this first phrase of forgiveness is completely unfathomable to our minds. How could someone forgive in the middle of this kind of darkness? And then we remember his words from his sermon: *"But I tell you who hear me: Love your enemies, do good to those who hate you, bless those who curse you, pray for those who mistreat you."* (Luke 6:27–8, NIV). We begin to understand their connection.

DEVOTIONAL PRAYER

Holy Jesus, Son of God, as we hear these words,

we confess that we are blind to the truth of your ways.

We are so earthbound in our need for fairness and justice

that it often keeps us holding onto hard places in our

hearts for years. Help us to see that "in your light,

we see light." Help us to let go of our pride that often hurts us

more than we know. Open our eyes to healing power of

your forgiveness so that we may let go of the things

that damage and wound us.

The Seven Last Words, Op. 51 (string quartet version), Joseph Haydn

Movement III: "Father forgive them..."

Emerson String Quartet, Deutsche Grammophon, 2004

Continue in prayerful consideration of his words. Hear the music of Haydn's string quartet *The Seven Last Words of Christ on the Cross* as it expresses, through the voice of the violin, the sweetness of Jesus' heart sharing a tender intimacy with the Father. Become a witness standing firm at the foot of the Cross. As you lean in to hear his words of forgiveness, block out all the ugliness of the crowd. Let the beauty of these words inspire your thoughts to forgive those who have falsely accused or insulted you in the past. Hold the picture of their faces in your mind, and let your heart fill with the desire to live in peace with those around us.

TODAY YOU SHALL BE
WITH ME IN PARADISE

Imagine yourself listening to all the sounds that surround Jesus as he is suffering on the Cross. Hear the taunting of the "chief priest, teachers of the law and elders" as they incite their people by saying, "He saved others; let him save himself if he is the Christ of God, the Chosen One" (v.35). Turn again and see the soldiers as they irreverently gamble for his clothing (v.34). Think about the ugliness of Golgotha, the place where Jesus innocently hung between two criminals. See him there in your mind's eye as the soldiers further humiliate him by placing the title "King of the Jews" over his head. They laugh and jeer at him, and the crowd grows in intensity to the point that even one of the thieves who hangs beside him joins their mocking voices.

But then a miracle: one of the thieves reaches out to Jesus in his moment of agony on the Cross. While all others are falsely accusing him, this unlikely one defends him by saying:

> *"...This man has done nothing wrong."* Then he said
> *"Jesus, remember me when you come into your kingdom."* [52]

And Jesus replies:

> *"Today you shall be with me in Paradise."* [53]

Imagine the heart of one who could show this kind of compassion. In a time when we all would be self-concerned, Jesus gives hope to another, and by doing this he shares the secret of creating positive, light-filled energy as a way to defy darkness. We are impressed with his ability to reach out in kindness to give hope to one of the thieves who hangs next to him, and we remember his earlier words, "Blessed are the merciful, for they will shown mercy" (Matthew 5:7, NIV).

DEVOTIONAL PRAYER

Gentle Savior, I am touched by your show of mercy as you

hung on the Cross; I celebrate that there was someone there

that day who acknowledged you as Savior.

Help us now in our lives to show compassion for

someone suffering, help us to see who that person is that

we must comfort by our presence. Give us the courage

to not look away from the ugly things in this world,

and let the knowledge of your ways inspire in us a desire

to reach out to others in our moment of darkness,

so that we will rise with renewed strength upon eagles' wings.

*C*ontinue in prayerful listening to the next musical selection.

Seven Last Words from the Cross,
James MacMillan

Movement III: "... today thou shalt be with me in paradise"

Graham Ross, Dmitri Ensemble, Naxos 2009

British composer James MacMillan has written this music so that we may experience the healing mystery of these words. Listen to how he does this by merging interlocking themes with eight voices singing in Latin:

> *Behold the Wood of the Cross, on which The Savior*
> *of the world was hung. Come let us adore him.*[54]

These voices are accompanied by string orchestra, slowly capturing the drama of the unveiling of the Cross during a Good Friday service. This verse is traditionally sung three times while the Cross is slowly revealed. To heighten the drama of this idea, MacMillan has the voices rise higher in pitch each time, like a slowly rising sun.

We turn again and listen to Jesus, now at his side so that we may understand his love with new eyes. Perhaps you are struggling with personal feelings of being misunderstood; listen as these voices express feelings of agony that come from the depth of suffering. Hold on and listen as the light of Jesus' voice, the violin, emerges through the pain. It grows louder and more intense as the idea of Jesus taking us to paradise dawns on our awareness. Share with Jesus the dark places in your heart, and lay down your burden so that you will be free to reach out to him. Focus on his forgiveness and let it heal your wounds. Trust in the sound of his voice. Let your voice join his now and begin to hear all the other voices who come to the Cross for grace and mercy.

BEHOLD YOUR SON;
BEHOLD YOUR MOTHER

"Near the Cross of Jesus stood his Mother..." (John 19:25)

Wait with me! Don't rush on to the listing of names that follow; just wait and really see Mary standing at the foot of the Cross, refusing to abandon her son. Thankfully, she is not alone; there are women who have stayed with her, knowing she would not leave her son; and then with her we see John, his beloved disciple, and we hear Jesus' voice again:

"Dear woman, here is your son," and he said to
the disciple "Here is your mother." [55]

We see in this moment the loving bond of a mother and son, and our hearts melt with compassion. We recall Jesus' words, "Blessed are those who mourn, for they will be comforted" (Matthew 5:4), but we must confess that we don't understand their wisdom. We want to wrap our arms around her to protect her from this unbearable moment.

DEVOTIONAL PRAYER

Sweet and tender Jesus, there is perhaps no sadder thought
than seeing your blessed mother standing near the Cross,
the mother who held you to her gentle breast and sang
you to sleep; who cared for your every need when
you were a tender boy. This blessed one now watches
in horror as your suffering also pierces her heart.

Grant that we may we become inspired by Mary's love.
Fill us with admiration for her courage,
and dedication to stand firmly at the foot of the Cross.
Help us understand this personally, and to see those
in our own lives that we must be present for, and share
in their burden. Let this inspire us to stand unmoved in the
face of suffering… and to become trustees of
your love towards one another and our fellow men.

Stabat Mater, G.B. Pergolesi

Movement I: Stabat Mater Dolorosa

Claudio Abbado, London Symphony Orchestra, Deutsche Grammophon 1990

Continue to realize this moment by prayerfully listening to the music of eighteenth-century Italian composer Giovanni Battista Pergolesi (1710–36), paired with the words of thirteenth-century Franciscan monk Jacopone di Todi. His poem *Stabat Mater Dolorosa* ("the sorrowful mother stood") was written to help us fully imagine Mary faithfully standing at the foot of the Cross.

At the Cross her station keeping,
Stood the mournful Mother weeping
Close to Jesus to the last

As the strings begin, we can hear the tension of the scene held in the upper pitches of the violins while the lower strings outline the harmonies and give the feeling of time passing. The choir enters with the same dissonant harmonies and we can imagine their young voices as those of the angels in heaven singing to comfort Mary, Jesus' mother, who rested him on her knee and held him to her breast. Visualize her as she must have stood by, watching and waiting for the end of his suffering.

MY GOD, MY GOD, WHY HAVE YOU FORSAKEN ME?

Now feel the loneliness of the Cross; remember how almost everyone had abandoned Jesus. One of his own disciples has betrayed him for a few pieces of silver; Peter, who once seemed so sure of his love, has now denied he ever knew him; all but his beloved disciple John have deserted him. Some of the same people who were praising Jesus as he entered Jerusalem only a week ago are now railing and hurling insults as he hangs naked on the Cross. He is experiencing a vortex of extreme physical, emotional, and spiritual pain, and so in the ninth hour of the day he expresses his deepest agony:

My God, my God, why have you forsaken me? [56]

Surely a darker moment has never passed among us. Think back to those first moments of Earth's inception when, before time began, "darkness was over the surface of the deep...." (Genesis 1:2). Wonder about the possibility of there being a time of complete darkness... a time when there is no light at all... no life-giving love from our creator.

Is there not something truly awe-inspiring about Jesus' cry of despair?

DEVOTIONAL PRAYER

Holy Rabbi, I can see here in your cry of despair your greatest teaching. In your hour of greatest suffering, you share with us your deepest moment of agony; in so doing, you share a type of intimacy with the Father that holds nothing back. You have reached into each of our hearts and expressed the inexpressible why… and we see there are mysteries even to you. And we remember your words: "Blessed are the poor in spirit, for theirs is the kingdom of heaven" (Matthew 5:3).

Thank you, Jesus, for showing us that asking questions and expressing our doubts and fears is part of the journey. Help us to trust that when we share our wounds with you, with God, the light of your love grows ever brighter. Because of your open suffering, we can see that you understand us when we feel separated from the Father and lost in darkness. Help us to remember and be strengthened in our faith by knowing our God, who loves us enough to go into darkness and let his Spirit "hover over the water" (see Genesis 1: 20) to create new life within us.

To highlight this moment further, continue in prayer while listening to the following movement of Haydn's great masterpiece.

The Seven Last Words of Christ (oratorio version), Joseph Haydn

Movement V: "Mein Gott"

Nikolaus Harnoncourt, Concentus Musicus Wien,

Arnold Schoenberg Choir, Elatus 2004

Imagine your voice joining this chorus as you consider this translation of their prayer, and as you do, let your heart connect to the feeling of the music portraying Jesus' moment of despair.

Why hast thou forsaken me?
Who can see God's work in this?
Who can grasp this mystery?
Oh God of strength and might,
Oh God of might and power,
We are the works of thy hands, and thy love,
　　oh Lord, has redeemed us.

Lord, we thank thee from our hearts.
For our sakes thou didst suffer pain, mockery,
　　abandonment, fear and torment.
Who could fail to love thee, Lord,
Who could sadden thee with sin?
Who could deny thy grace?
No, Nothing shall part us from thee,
　　here and in eternity

I THIRST

We cannot really understand the horrible physical pain Jesus endured on the Cross. As we witness this event, our mind numbs at the thought of each physical challenge he faced. We see him in the garden as he prayed with such anguish "his sweat was like drops of blood" (Luke 22:44). Arrested and put on trial in the middle of the night, Jesus faces the Cross already exhausted and dehydrated. He is beaten, then scourged by a Roman legionnaire using a device that tears at his flesh, leaving the skin on his back, legs, and shoulders in shredded strips. He is then forced to carry his Cross, weighing approximately 110 pounds, over a distance of 650 yards, to the place of execution. He falls under the weight of it several times until they force a man from the crowd to carry it for him. Jesus, weak and bleeding, follows. He is then nailed to the Cross.

Over the hours that follow we hear him utter just a few last phrases. Each of these thoughts are exceptionally hard for him to utter, because every breath he takes is a slow excruciating process of pushing himself upward allowing the full weight of his body to press against the nails in his feet so that he might quickly inhale. Because of this, his mouth becomes extremely dry; that alone is an agony for him.

"I am thirsty." [57]

DEVOTIONAL PRAYER

Loving Jesus, we see your suffering and we feel helpless. We feel ashamed of a humanity who could invent such a horror-filled death. Jesus, the perfect Lamb of God who takes away the sins of the world, we see your suffering for love of us, and we want to turn away. In this moment of the Cross, guide our thoughts to look deeply and unflinchingly at your thirst.

Strengthen us so that we may open our eyes to the ongoing suffering of others in the world. Help us now to have your love for the stranger, those who hunger, the lonely in prison, as we remember your words: "For I was hungry and you gave me something to eat, I was thirsty and you gave me something to drink, I was a stranger and you invited me in, I needed clothes and you clothed me, I was sick and you looked after me, I was in prison and you came to visit me" (Matthew: 25:35—6, NIV).

*C*ontinue to prayerfully listen.

Seven Last Words from the Cross, James MacMillan

Movement 5: "I thirst"

Graham Ross, Dmitri Ensemble, Naxos 2009

The music begins very quietly, tension-filled chords allowing us to float above the scene to observe Jesus' suffering from a distance. The desolation portrayed by the music helps us feel the unrelenting heat of the atmosphere. We can imagine Jesus drifting in and out of consciousness, and as the music crescendos we feel the agony of his thirst, growing each time we hear him crying out.

Then we hear the voices whisper the ideas that might have drifted through his mind. *"I gave you to drink of life-giving water from the rock; and you gave me to drink of gall and vinegar."* [58] Let his open expression of need build to a great crescendo of desire in all of us. Help us, as we seek to see Jesus' face in those who are thirsty for love.

IT IS FINISHED

Jesus is tired, struggling for his final breaths. He is longing to go but lingering with us and finally he gives in to the crushing weight of his mortality and utters:

"It is finished." [59]

DEVOTIONAL PRAYER

*Words cannot describe our feelings of loss at this moment of
your death. You—God Incarnate—who walked among us so that
you might experience fully the pain of our humanity, are gone.
Your light has been extinguished. Help us to see, with our inner eyes
of faith, the amazing nature of a God willing to go through everything,
for the love of us. Rest now from all your suffering; we hold on
to the idea of there being and ending to all pain.*

*Help us to feel the wisdom of the phrase "It is finished" personally.
When we have agony, remind us of your words, and help us hold on
to the light of knowing that all suffering ends. Even though we have
knowledge of your victorious resurrection to come, allow us to view
this moment of the Cross; let us renew our gratitude for
your sacrifice and learn how to let go of our own struggling.*

As we mourn for Jesus' broken heart, the beauty of his ways expressed in this music comforts us.

The Seven Last Words of Christ (oratorio version), Joseph Haydn

Movement VI: Introduction Two,

Nikolaus Harnoncourt, Concentus Musicus Wien,

Arnold Schoenberg Choir, Elatus 2004

Let the glorious nature of this music work to purify your heart so that Jesus' spirit will be born to live again in each of us, and so that you may honor him by living in harmony and fellowship with those around you.

FATHER, INTO YOUR HANDS I COMMIT MY SPIRIT

Learning to trust is perhaps the most difficult of the Seven Words to put into practice. Because of this, we stand amazed in the presence of Jesus' gentle spirit as he speaks this last phrase.

"Father into your hands I commit my spirit."
When he had said this he breathed his last. [60]

We pause now in a moment of silence—no words can express our sorrow at the thought of a time when your light was extinguished from our view.

Slowly let go of this final scene; allow it to fade from your mind as you remember Jesus' preaching, and see the wisdom of his words with new eyes:

Therefore everyone who hears these words of mine and puts them
into practice is like a wise man who built his house on the rock.
The rain came down, the streams rose, and the winds blew and beat against
the house; yet it did not fall, because it had its foundation on the rock. [61]

DEVOTIONAL PRAYER

Loving Father, Obedient Son, and Comforting

Holy Spirit, let us hear in these your last words

from the Cross your plan for all our lives.

Grant us now that we may find peace in our lives.

Help us let go of our need to control the outcome

of everything, and to see more fully that you paid

the ultimate price for our salvation. Let the wisdom of

your words show us how to rest in the Father's care.

In your blessed and holy name, we live and breathe.

Amen.

Die Sieben Worte Jesu Christi am Kreuz,
Heinrich Schütz (1585–1672)

Movements 9, 10, and 11

Paul Hillier, Ars Nova Copenhagen, Dacapo 2010

As you listen to these beautiful short choruses by German composer Heinrich Schütz, return to the *Crucifixion* image of jm-ART and begin to piece together all the perspectives you have experienced during these meditations. Let these multi-dimensional reflections merge into one lasting impression that you can return to, knowing it will always be there, flowing with a powerful healing stream of creative light.

With Jesus' last phrases he shows us how to be meek, compassionate, forgiving. He shows us how to ask for what we need and demonstrates the comfort we will find when we enlarge our family. But he also shares with us the freedom to express our deepest questions of despair.

When we really see the way of the Cross, our hearts melt, because we finally realize our true need for this sacrifice... our truth. In Jesus' passion of the Cross we see inside the very heart of God. And as we gaze in wonder, we see with new eyes the beauty of it all, and we no longer hide our faces in shame. Instead we fix our eyes on his glory, because we know that God does not promise us a life without suffering; what he does instead is suffer with us. *Emmanuel*—God is with us, holding us and guiding us through the suffering... and it is more than enough.

REFLECT & JOURNAL

Take a moment and journal about what you found surprising during your time listening at the foot of the cross. What did you discover, and how have you been changed?

Read Revelation 5:1—13 and imagine sharing John's vision of a new song:

*Then I saw a Lamb, looking as if it had been slain,
standing in the center of the throne, encircled by the four
living creatures and the elders... He came and took the scroll
from the right hand of him who sat on the throne.*[62]

To deepen your consideration of the presence of God at the Cross,
search the Wikimedia Commons for:
❖ *Adoration of the Trinity (Landauer Altarpiece), 1509—11, Albrecht Dürer*
❖ *Holy Trinity, (Basilica of Santa Maria Novella), 1425, Masaccio*

CHAPTER EIGHT

WHY ARE YOU DOWNCAST, O MY SOUL?

(PSALM 42:5)

All shall be well, and all shall be well

and all manner of thing shall be well.

—JULIAN OF NORWICH

AVE VERUM CORPUS

Hail, true Body, born of the Virgin Mary,

who having truly suffered, was sacrificed

on the cross for mankind,

whose pierced side flowed with water and blood:

May it be for us a foretaste [of the Heavenly banquet]

in the trial of death.

O sweet Jesus, O holy Jesus,

O Jesus, son of Mary, have mercy on me.

Amen.

—FOURTEENTH-CENTURY EUCHARISTIC HYMN,

ATTRIBUTED TO POPE INNOCENT VI

Holy Saturday is a special day set aside for quiet reflection by Coptic Christians, Eastern Orthodox, Roman Catholics, Anglicans, Episcopalians, Lutherans, and Methodists. These fellowships will, in a variety of poignant ways, mark the time between Good Friday and Easter Sunday so they might remember the precise moment of Christ's death and the following hours while he was buried in the tomb. Some will strip the cross of its adornments, while others will shroud this symbol of sacrifice in black. The Lutherans abstain from the use of music, so that its reintroduction will have a greater feeling of grand pageantry at daybreak. Roman Catholics withhold the distribution of the Blessed Sacrament until after sundown on Saturday, so they might reintroduce his body and blood during their Easter Vigil. This Mass dramatically opens with the darkening of their church as they await the entrance of a single flame of light, representing Jesus as the light of the world and the glorious hope we find in his resurrection on Easter morning.

Why do so many church traditions immerse themselves in these customs of silence and lamentation? What is the benefit of reliving the time when Jesus was in the grave? Why do they foster traditions that lead their faith community towards a feeling of heart-pounding anticipation? As I was brought up an outsider to these observances of the liturgical calendar, I still feel a bit self-conscious when it comes to all the regalia of traditional colors and ornamentation commonly used to guide the prayers of the mainstream Christian community. I have learned, however, that these traditions hold mysterious benefit, and are valued because they lead their community into a richer connection with each other and, in turn, with God. And so, instead of shrugging them off as meaningless encumbrances, I remain open and curious to these time-honored practices.

Since we have recognized that God is always with us, demonstrating his profound love for us by sacrificing himself through his son Jesus Christ, I ask again: what can it benefit us to meditate further on his descent from the Cross? How does viewing these first disciples tenderly caring and grieving over Jesus' broken body provide valuable spiritual food for our journey towards becoming more like Christ?

Perhaps the best place to find our meaning is by listening to the way Jesus used metaphors in preparing his first disciples for his impending death. By doing this, he gently directs all of us to think on his sacrifice as a seed that must give itself to the process of bringing new life.

I tell you the truth, unless a kernel of wheat falls to the ground and dies, it remains only a single seed. But if it dies, it produces many seeds. [63]

He then connects us to becoming offspring of God's love to the world when he says:

Put your trust in the light while you have it, so that you may become sons of light. [64]

In *The Way of the Cross*, Caryll House-lander reflects on this period of Jesus' silence as a time of mysterious gestation for the world. She poetically inspires us with her interpretation of Jesus' words when she expresses:

… never has there been a night in the whole history of mankind so pregnant with the secret of the unending life and joy that was to break upon the world with the dawn. [65]

The idea of Jesus' death leading to our rejuvenation is attractive; it teases our thoughts back to our genesis, and reminds us of the nature of God, who miraculously created the world out of nothingness. Houselander continues:

[When] Christ was in the tomb; the whole world was sown with the seed of Christ's life… in the womb of the whole world… in order that His life should quicken in countless hearts, over and over again for all time. [66]

Just as God lovingly created life in the beginning, our spirits are inexplicably renewed each year as we view Jesus' sacrifice. It is by experiencing his death and burial that we are led to our new creation.

How does viewing this scene change us, and how will grieving over Jesus' body nurture a closer connection with God? Why should Jesus die so that we might live? How should we focus our thoughts into a deeper understanding of what is happening during this time when Jesus was in the grave?

Much of what Paul wrote in his letters to the various early churches is dedicated to explaining the reason for Christ's death. And yet it is Peter who seems to stir up the most controversy when he wrote that during this time, Jesus "preached to the spirits in prison who disobeyed long ago" (I Peter 3:19–20).

This single passage, inspiring at least eighteen varied interpretations,[67] has been the reason for the inclusion of the line "died, and was buried; he descended into hell..." in the Apostles' Creed. Traditionally referred to as "Christ's Harrowing of Hell," this interpretation was accepted as early as the fourth century, and is still regularly recited as part of the declaration of the major tenets of the Christian faith. Because of this, artists have regularly included rather macabre paintings of Jesus crashing through the gates of hell to release those imprisoned in darkness by demons. And yet even Augustine (A.D. 354–430) questioned this interpretation of Christ literally descending into hell and believed it to be more "allegory than history." [68]

I must confess, I prefer to think of Jesus as resting from his suffering during this time. Because our Christian heritage is deeply rooted in the Hebrew tradition, it seems right to have this relaxation during the Sabbath. Just as God rested after creating the world, Jesus rests from his labor on Saturday. In viewing his burial during the annual observations of Holy Week, we are reminded to rest and to wait for his resurrection. I am content in viewing this event as a mystery, and I accept the practice of respite on Holy Saturday as something that will give rise to new insights for me over my lifetime.

However, there is still a part of me that wonders about the need for his death. Not having grown up in times of sacrificial blood offerings, I must admit I still have a lot of unanswered questions. My curiosity on the subject eventually led me into conversation with my friend Brandon Fredenburg, Assistant Professor of Bible Studies at Lubbock Christian University. With his guidance, I was led to a theory that gives me a new sense of wonder at the amazing nature of God's love for us. Archbishop Hilarion Alfeyev of the Russian Orthodox Church, teacher of theology and New Testament Studies at the Moscow Theological Academy, explains this passage in I Peter as a time when Jesus defied Satan's darkness:

> *[God] Himself became man, suffered on the Cross and died, descended into Hades and was raised from the dead in order to share human fate. By descending into Hades, Christ did not destroy the devil as a personal, living creature, but 'abolished the power of the devil,' that is, deprived the devil of authority and power stolen by him*

*from God. When he rebelled against God, the devil set himself the task to create his own autonomous kingdom where he would be master and where he would win back from God **a space where God's presence could be in no way felt.** In Old Testament understanding, this place was Sheol. After Christ, Sheol became a place of divine presence.*[69] *[emphasis added]*

Thinking on such deep theological matters does give us pause. Meditation on the mysterious nature of God, who loved us so that he sacrificed his divine light in order that he might bring his sons and daughters to glory, fills my heart with love and renews my deep need for seeing Jesus.

I am reminded of a lovely legend adopted by early Christians from pre-Christian times that tells of the unrestrained love of the mother pelican. In times of great famine the pelican was said to wound her breast by tearing at the flesh so that she might feed her chicks with her life-giving blood. Early Christians, touched by this story, began to use the pelican as a symbol to express the very nature of God. Because of this, you can still find the self-sacrificing symbol of the pelican embed into altars containing the communion bread and wine, the Blessed Sacrament of our Lord.

The use of this symbol speaks volumes to the power of images, and how they can bind us together with a single brush stroke more effectively than a thousand words. I can see the power of God's plan to recapture our hearts with Jesus' sacrifice on the cross as an event that would gracefully speak of his unending love for us. It is when we fully observe God's action on our behalf that we begin to desire him, and pledge our lives so that we might commune with him. With the suffering and sacrifice of his son, he cancels out all the misunderstanding of man's original sin in the garden and eternally woos our soul, calling us back from all our hiding.

ART: *Rogier van der Weyden,*
The Descent from the Cross, 1435—38.

Oil on panel, 86.6 x 103.1 inches.

Prado Museum, Madrid, Spain.

ROGIER VAN DER WEYDEN:
The Descent from the Cross

Before contemplating Jesus' burial, we will let our hearts dwell on the visual reminders of those disciples who cared for Jesus' precious body in the first moments after his death. To do this, we will gather around Flemish artist Rogier van der Weyden's painting *The Descent from the Cross.*

This masterpiece, commissioned by Greater Guild of Crossbowmen of Louvain for the Chapel of Our Lady Without the Walls, offers many small touches that can stimulate the imagination. Note that the artist paid homage to his patrons by placing the body of the crucified Christ in the shape of a crossbow, a shape echoed in the delicately painted ornamental corners. Armed with the knowledge that I am in the presence of a painting loaded with symbolic meaning, I respectfully delve deeper, knowing there will be more such hidden treasures to come.

Weyden masterfully highlights the multifaceted character of Christ and beautifully portrays each mourner with lavish details that refer to the personal stories of their conversions. The intricate folds of their garments, the individualized coloring of their faces, and their carefully choreographed poses all work like a symphony of expression, woven together to entice us to commune with them in their grief. Each life-sized figure is handsomely crafted to create the illusion of varying degrees of depth, suggesting a new kind of full-color relief sculpture. Mary swoons, Nicodemus cradles, Joseph of Arimathea attends, Mary Magdalene worships; and Weyden carefully directs this action held within a single frame, placing Jesus' disciples on a proscenium stage so that we might view them from a safe distance—or so we might think. But the longer you gaze at this artistry, the intensity and visual impact of each figure increases as Weyden subtly draws your eyes deeper into the story.

After you have lingered with Weyden's masterpiece, read over the passage recorded in John 19:38–42 outlining the details of Jesus' burial, and take a moment to identify the different figures in the painting.

Ave Verum Corpus, Mozart

"Ave verum corpus," which in Latin means, "Hail, true body" (the phrase concludes with "born of the Virgin Mary") is a fourteenth-century Eucharistic hymn often attributed to Pope Innocent VI, originally sung during the consecration of the host for communion. It is frequently set to music by composers; one such famous setting is Mozart's poignant motet *Ave Verum Corpus* K. 618. Close your eyes and allow yourself to be reverently carried into the scene as you listen.

Agnus Dei II: Music to Soothe the Soul

Track 4, "Ave Verum Corpus" K. 618, W.A. Mozart,

Edward Higginbottom, Choir of New College Oxford,

Erato Disques 1999

It is interesting to consider and compare each of the gospel accounts as they highlight slightly different perspectives of the event. However, John was an important eyewitness on the scene, and so his account seems richer; we remind ourselves that he was actually there and therefore writing from his firsthand experience of events.

Later, Joseph of Arimathea asked Pilate for the body of Jesus. Now Joseph was a disciple of Jesus, but secretly because he feared the Jews. With Pilate's permission, he came and took the body away. He was accompanied by Nicodemus, the man who earlier had visited Jesus at night. Nicodemus brought a mixture of myrrh and aloes, about seventy-five pounds. Taking Jesus' body, the two of them wrapped it, with the spices, in strips of linen. This was in accordance with Jewish burial customs. At the place where Jesus was crucified, there was a garden, and in the garden a new tomb, in which no one had ever been laid. Because it was the Jewish day of Preparation and since the tomb was nearby, they laid Jesus there.[70]

Before you continue your exploration of this painting, take a moment to consider Weyden's assembly of characters found in the various gospel accounts. Can you imagine him standing before a blank canvas, wondering how to begin? I wonder what his process might have been in deciding how to represent the faithful group who attended Jesus that day. How would you decide to paint them, in your mind's eye?

Notice how Weyden represents this scene in a very realistic space. There are no golden halos or floating angels; instead he whimsically chooses to accentuate the physical reality by candidly capturing the moment the young man, squeezed at the top of the ladder, catches his robe on the corner of the delicately painted traceries.

*N*ow that you have taken the time to consider your own reflections on Jesus' burial, we will begin again by reading the painting from left to right, like a storybook. Considering first the overall composition of the painting, we note there are ten participants incorporated into three groupings of figures.

In the left group, Weyden portrays those who are caring for Mary as she is overcome with emotional distress upon the death of her son. The portrayal of Jesus' mother swooning has been a traditional embellishment to the story of Mary faithfully staying with him, unable to separate herself from her son's suffering. Representing her this way has become a permanent fixture in her iconography; it allows us to vividly imagine the exact moment, as Simeon predicted, when a sword pierced her soul (see Luke 2:35). Even though Mary's swoon is not recorded in scripture, the idea of this gesture captures the heartrending sweep of emotion she must have felt at the time of Jesus' passing.

Weyden represents Mary's spiritual connection to Jesus' suffering by echoing his posture, positioning her with her arms awkwardly spread out. In doing this he plants the idea in our hearts that Mary, too, was near death after witnessing her son's suffering for hours. We are comforted at the sight of John the beloved, tending to Mary as Jesus requested. With him are two other women, possibly Mary of Cleophas (downcast in the back), and Mary of Salome (in green), who are traditionally thought to be Mary's half-sisters. Viewing this group, we can silently praise and honor these women who unflinchingly stayed with Mary. Her presence at the foot of the Cross and subsequent swoon reminds of the baby Jesus who was the "Light of the World" and we can grieve over the knowledge that for a brief time his light was extinguished from our view.

In the center, Christ's body is stretched out and presented to us in full view as it is heavily borne by two men: Nicodemus, in a jewel-trimmed red robe, and Joseph of Arimathea in a richly designed fur-trimmed robe. A third man, possibly one of Joseph's servants, holds a jar of precious spices behind him. With this Weyden reminds us of the three wise men who presented precious gifts of frankincense and myrrh to the baby Jesus as they knelt and worshipped at his feet. Here we see that Jesus' story has come full circle, and we are reminded that the infant, who was first laid in a manger, will now lay his sacred head in a borrowed tomb.

We can admire Joseph of Arimathea as we see him stepping forward to provide Jesus with the costly spices needed to prepare his body for burial. What we know of him from the gospels is brief. Matthew describes him as the "rich man from Arimathea... who had himself become a disciple of Jesus" (Matthew 27:57). However, Mark introduces him as "a prominent member of the counsel," presumably the Jewish Sanhedrin (Mark 15:43), and John tells that he has been fearful of the Jewish leaders and so he was a disciple only "secretly."

Weyden beautifully illustrates Joseph's change of heart, painting his clothes with an ostentatious display of color. His sumptuous robe, heavily embroidered with a gold-threaded flower pattern, is a feast for our eyes. Joseph's great wealth is suggested through a variety of textures including sable, silk, velvet, and linen. During Weyden's lifetime, this "field-of-the-cloth-gold" fabric was used as an expression of power and grandeur during peace negotiations on the battlefield, and was often draped as a canopy over a prince's throne. Knowing this adds another dimension to Weyden's devotion. The rich, detailed clothing sweeps us in, and we at last discover Joseph's tear-stained face. Lingering, we imagine the heart of this man we know so little of, and how he played such an

important role by stepping out of the shadows to care for and honor our Prince of Peace.

As for Nicodemus, we have the advantage of an entire conversation recorded in the third chapter of John's Gospel, which provocatively describes him visiting Jesus "by night." When he arrives to help in the deposition of Jesus' body, we can celebrate his moment of stepping out of darkness, and we hear the words of Jesus echoing:

> But whoever lives by the truth comes
> into the light, so that it may be
> seen plainly that what he has done
> has been done through God.[71]

Weyden hints at the change in Nicodemus by dressing him from head to toe in red, and having him covered and clothed with the body of Christ. To witness his conversion is to see the possibility for our own transformation when we accept the broken body of Christ, and so the presence of Nicodemus at the Cross reminds us of how Jesus brings us into the light by being our "wonderful counselor."

On the far right of the painting, Mary Magdalene is dramatically posed as she focuses intently on the sacred wounds in Jesus' feet. As we meditate on her zealous gesture, we are again reminded of a transformation story. While Mary Magdalene is frequently mentioned in the lists of those present at the defining moments of Jesus' life, these references merely describe her as the woman Jesus healed by casting out seven demons (see Luke 8:2). We can only imagine the spiritual torment she must have endured. Because Jesus released her from physical, spiritual, and emotional pain, she becomes one of his most faithful disciples, giving him not only emotional but also financial support.

However, because she is mentioned in close relation to the story of the woman who washed Jesus' feet with her tears and dried them with her hair (see Luke 7:36-50), she is often cast as a sinful woman or reformed prostitute. This part of her story, attached to her only in the Middle Ages, inspired artists to often portray her with long, flowing hair in a type of unrestrained display of grief at the foot of the Cross; she will eternally be the woman who gazes and weeps over Jesus' nail-scarred feet. Her presence at the Cross, and her dedication to the wounds on his feet, reminds us that Jesus' blood frees us from the guilt of our sins. We can use the sight of her to help guide our thoughts towards a greater experience of Jesus as the "friend of sinners" and the "great physician."

Each time you come to Weyden's great painting, there are new insights to uncover. Just as Jesus' story is retold every year in the cycle of the liturgical calendar, this painting repeatedly calls to us, like church bells ringing to gather us in so that we might stand once more on holy ground. In a similar way, fourteenth-century Christian writer Thomas à Kempis, in his devotions on the Passion of Christ, tenderly expresses his love for our Lord as he imagines himself aiding those first disciples as they took Jesus' broken body from the Cross. As we read his words, our hearts can reach out and join with him. We are bonded by our mutual love of Christ, and we become a fellowship stretching across time:

> *Would that I, the least of all servants*
> *of God, had been present at the burial*
> *of my Lord, so that I could have*
> *offered him some service, no matter*
> *how slight. I certainly would willingly*
> *have held the ladder next to the Cross*
> *or handed up the instruments used to*
> *pull out the nails or given a helping*
> *hand to those holding the body.[72]*

Spending time in reflection of Jesus' burial through a meditation of this painting feeds our spirit because as we linger with these disciples who are grieving over the death of their beloved teacher and friend, we become a community bonded by our mutual love of Christ. When our hearts are pricked at the sight of Jesus' torn body, we become impassioned over all suffering that darkness impartially inflicts upon the world. Viewing Jesus' suffering and ultimate death reminds us that in every new birth, there is pain. Knowing this, we are moved once again to rekindle God's light. These are the images that cause us to defy the darkness as we step out of our comfortable places in the shadows to pick up the light of our Lord... and when we do, we grab hold of a fresh hope in God's goodness, igniting a spark of new life.

REFLECT & JOURNAL

If you like, take a moment to pause and journal, creating a prayer that expresses a deep concern you might be trying to carry on your own. Because I needed help with learning how to pray in times of sorrow, I found comfort in the following advice from Chris Altrock's Prayers From the Pit: Learning to Pray in Times of Pain. I offer it to you as a guide through your own "tough times":

*Pray with **expectation** that what God is beginning he will also bring to an end. Pray with **anticipation** that the God who's called you to this work will indeed walk through it with you. Pray with **conviction** that he will see it to the end. Pray with **exultation** for the way God brought fulfillment to that task. Pray with thanksgiving and praise for the way that season of winter is now over and spring is becoming visible. Pray with **gratitude**....[73] [emphasis added]*

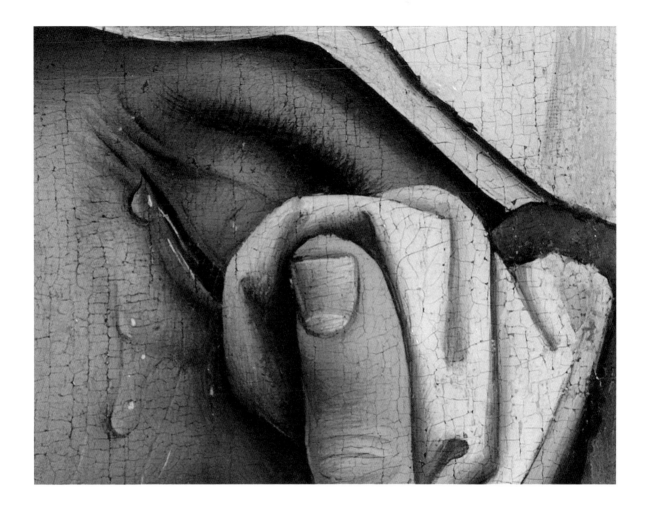

ART: *Descent from the Cross*

(detail: Stabat Mater (Mary), left; tears)

As I was considering the importance of really seeing and experiencing these disciples who surrounded Jesus at his death and burial, I was drawn to observe this compelling close-up of a single tear. Before I faced my own pain, I silently paused to give thanks for the mastery of this artist's hand and his genius in capturing the exquisiteness of a single tear... it is breathtaking. And as I gazed at the refracted skin seen through the teardrop, I treasured this close-up as a holy relic of sorrow from an early disciple who stayed with the body of my Savior.

In reflection, I connected with this woman's sadness; it took me deep within myself. Lingering with her grief reminded me of the many burdens I have carried within my soul. Her unguarded outpouring of emotion prompted me to recall the storms of tears I have shed that have kept me from seeing my way forward. There is real suffering in her tear, and it caused me to shake my head and wonder at the need for Jesus' sacrifice once more. Even so, gazing at her tears caused me to remember those times when I felt I had lost God... those times when I had forgotten how to pray.

But then I noticed that captured within the tear was something I had not seen at first. Hidden there was the secret that made it possible to see the pain within her tear, frozen in time... and this great mystery was the essence of *light*.

I realized anew that the way forward is to focus on the light of God's love. To open myself to this thought and to trust in his ways... this is the light that will transform my grief to joy. And like the rising of a new dawn, I began to see that to fully embrace the light, I must first allow it to help me release the darkness.

I must fearlessly cast off the old ways of thinking so that I can welcome new horizons. I must bury my guilt and regret so that I will no longer be loaded down by the weight of my despair. When I trust that God will be glorified in all his ways I can let go of my worry of hurting others, because I know that in all things, God is calling me forward to his good purposes. Because of this, I can lay to rest my need for acceptance and praise, and learn to hear God's call for my life more clearly.

In our imitation of Christ, we must realize our need to willingly leave behind the prescribed ways of this world so that we might pick up Jesus' Way of the Cross. Observing and remembering Holy Saturday annually reminds us that our progress toward new life involves putting away something old. Because of this, I have new understanding of the letters of Paul when he writes:

We always carry around in our body the death of Jesus, so that
the life of Jesus may also be revealed in our body. For we who
are alive are always being given over to death for Jesus' sake,
so that his life maybe revealed in our mortal body.[74]

The key here is that before the joy of the resurrection, we must each individually let our heart be torn with grief over the loss of light in a world of darkness. Before I am moved to sacrifice my comfort, my self-seeking ways, my clinging to social norms, I need to see the need for my participation in the light.

In viewing the lamentation of Christ, I can take my mind back to a time when the disciples faced the horror of a dark humanity, which for a brief time extinguished the divine light of the world. When we see them in their grief and recognize it as akin to those dark places we cling to within ourselves—we become ignited with a new desire for God's light.

Our call, then, is to answer fear, ignorance, prejudice, and injustice by volunteering to join our light to the resistance against the darkness, each of us in our own quiet ways. And when we do, we become like a gentle breeze blowing to give new life to the flames of love our Father has planted within us.

This morning, as I write these closing thoughts, I have just returned from visiting a Sunday service at one of the many historic churches in downtown Frederick, Maryland. These people have been recent supporters of mine, and even though the place I call home has vastly different ways of praising God and celebrating the life of our Lord, I have for a time become grafted into their branch of discipleship by our mutual dedication to the story of Jesus.

Today as their pastor spoke he openly shared with us that his family had been experiencing "tough times," and from the tone of his statement I quickly understood that he had been grieving, that there had been a sudden death in the family that he was still processing.

Despite his grief, I was amazed at how he was able to craft a lesson that touched us in a memorable way. It had humor; he painted pictures; he was personal; he tied us beautifully to our historical past; and, while he was speaking, I realized he was healing and burying his pain. As we listened to him, we provided him with the opportunity to find meaning in his personal sorrow that would give him the strength to join himself once again to our community of light. In those few moments, he was able to step down from his pulpit to openly share his vulnerability, and as he spoke he became one of us. His story became our story, and we were bonded together by our care for one another and our mutual faith in Jesus' light as a presence in this world.

After the service I turned to my newfound friend and fellow art lover Judy Bergeson, and asked why she thought it important to spend time in reflection of Jesus' death during Holy Saturday. With eyes wide open, she quickly replied, "It's simple! Because when we see his death, we know he was really *human*... but then, oh my—just wait until we see what happens next!"

As I walked away with her words still ringing in my ears, I thought, *Yep, it's simple really... Jesus was human, and just wait until we see what happens next!*

For more paintings by Rogier van der Weyden, search Wikimedia Commons for:

❖ *The Seven Sacraments altarpiece (1445—50)*

❖ *The Crucifixion, with the Virgin and St. John the Evangelist Mourning (1460)*

CHAPTER NINE

DO YOU BELIEVE THIS?

(JOHN 11:26B)

God is gone up on high with a triumphant noise.

—CHARLES WESLEY

CHRIST THE LORD IS RISEN TODAY

Christ the Lord is ris'n today, Alleluia!

Sons of men and angels say, Alleluia!

Raise your joys and triumphs high, Alleluia!

Sing, ye heav'ns, and earth, reply, Alleluia

Love's redeeming work is done, Alleluia!

Fought the fight, the battle won, Alleluia!

Death in vain forbids His rise, Alleluia!

Christ hath opened paradise, Alleluia!

Soar we now where Christ hath led, Alleluia!

Foll'wing our exalted Head, Alleluia!

Made like Him, like Him we rise, Alleluia!

Ours the cross, the grave, the skies, Alleluia!

King of glory, Soul of bliss, Alleluia!

Everlasting life is this, Alleluia!

Thee to know, Thy pow'r to prove, Alleluia!

Thus to sing, and thus to love, Alleluia!

—CHARLES WESLEY (1739)

Early on the first day of the week, while it was still dark...[75]

Since we have always lived as "first day of the week" people, it is challenging for us to step back in time to understand the feelings of those who first heard the words "He has risen!" Having always known this angel's proclamation as a source of our spiritual identity, our truth, it is difficult to imagine ourselves inside the experience of those women who were first to arrive on the scene the morning of Jesus' Resurrection. But if we long to give birth to the light of Jesus so he might unfold his living presence in our daily lives, I believe we must experience the joy and wonder of his Resurrection right down to our toes. To do this, we will once more immerse ourselves in the darkness so we might allow the slow dawning of the knowledge of God's love within our hearts.

Music has the power to trigger our emotions with a language that universally touches our hearts, and so I have carefully selected three pieces to explore the reactions of the first disciples in a sort of "grand resurrection trilogy." Like the soundtrack of a movie, this music will carry you deeper into the events so that you might walk among those first believers. As you listen to these masterpieces, you will experience a slow rise of excitement, then a sudden burst of joy, culminating with a full-flowering, glorious transfiguration. As you allow yourself to be completely immersed in sound, the music will become a bridge for your senses, helping you travel back in time. In this way, you can transcend to a greater emotional connection with the reality of Jesus' Resurrection.

This is the good news! *Jesus rose again!* And he continues to enliven himself among us, as our individual knowledge of our eternal life in him regenerates and transforms our lives.

RETUNING OUR THOUGHTS

Begin to open your thoughts to the feelings of discovery by thinking of a time in your life when the activities of an ordinary day were suddenly suspended, as your awareness abruptly collided with news that shook you to your core. Think of a time when your perception of the world was changed in an instant, whether it was a personal trauma or a news event of cataclysmic proportions. As you think on these things, try to harness the feelings that are still buried deep in your subconscious mind. Fine-tune your emotional response until you sympathetically vibrate at the same frequency as did the women stunned by an extraordinary vision of angels early that Sunday morning.

N.T. Wright, in *Scripture and the Authority of God: How to Read the Bible Today*, advises us towards these kinds of imaginative exercises as a healthy way to connect with sacred scriptures:

A familiar story told with a twist in the tail jolts people into thinking differently about themselves and the world. A story told with pathos, humor or drama opens the imagination and invites the readers and hearers to imagine themselves in similar situations, offering new insights about God and human beings which enable them to order their own lives more wisely.[76]

David A. Seamands, in *Healing for Damaged Emotions*, metaphorically likens our emotional responses to events as the growth history found in the rings of a tree:

In the rings of our thoughts and emotions the record is there; the memories are recorded, and all are alive. And they directly and deeply affect our concepts, our feelings, our relationships... [These deeply embedded emotions] affect the way we look at life and God, at others and ourselves.[77]

Generating an emotional response—or as we might say, "getting in touch with our feelings"—helps us to become more alive to the scenes outlined in the Bible. It is when we allow ourselves to tap into the emotional history carried deep within our hearts that we begin to connect to the story of Jesus *personally*. His Resurrection becomes a part of our identity and transforms the way we react to the events of our day. As we open our hearts to listen for God's message, we allow His spirit to give us the spark of miraculous conception that will in turn give birth to new life.

To highlight an example of the kind of Spirit-led reflection I am referring to: Recently I developed a fuller understanding of the Resurrection as I was inadvertently drawn into a documentary detailing the events surrounding the assassination of President John F. Kennedy.

Since I do not have a direct memory of this dramatic day, I have always been fascinated by the stories of ordinary people who, despite the distance of years, can tell you exactly what they were doing when they heard the news of Kennedy's shooting. The event was so earth-shattering for them that their memories are still vibrantly alive. They can tell you where they were, what they were doing, even the song that might have been playing on the radio. These seemingly minor details have everlastingly imprinted a situated meaning on their mind that can instantly carry them back in time, allowing them to relive this extraordinary day. If you are in the presence of a good storyteller, their accounting of their experience can allow you to join with them as they step back in time.

In this way, my feelings for the tragedy were heightened even further by this documentary, upon hearing news reporters give minute-by-minute accounts as they relived the details of anxiously working to confirm reports of President Kennedy's death so they might break the traumatic news to the American public.

JFK had become an icon to the American people, who gathered nightly to view idyllic scenes of his young family casually playing on the White House lawn. Scenes of domestic bliss had regularly been projected into the nation's living rooms, and reporters knew the announcement of his death would be devastating. The relatively new invention of the television had created an unprecedented emotional connection to the image of his presidency, reinvigorating the American dream of leading the world into a prosperous future as a kind of utopian society.

Not willing to let go of their visions of perfection, reporters' minds quickly careened through all the possible outcomes for the day. Fearing the worst, several excruciating minutes passed as they attempted to contact the Dallas police, then the hospital, and finally various reporters near the scene so they might accurately air the news to the public. It is hard for us to imagine, as we all now carry cell phones which give us the capability of live video, but when the White House finally made their official announcement, it was to a handful of reporters who then ran down the hall to grab one of the few available pay phones to call in the news. All of this frantic activity took place so that someone might quietly hand Walter Cronkite the following Associated Press bulletin to read on air:

From Dallas, Texas, the flash, apparently official: "PRESIDENT KENNEDY DIED AT 1 P.M. (CST)," 2:00 Eastern Standard Time, some thirty-eight minutes ago.

I can imagine Cronkite quickly reading over the news flash, his mind racing to find the right words. Still struggling to adjust to the news he is about to announce, he adds "apparently official" as one last attempt to soften the blow. Reading and imagining the tone and rhythm of his words sends a chill down my spine. The impact of these few, staccato words run straight through me, as I think of how the stark reality of this announcement must have hit the American public like a slap in the face.

Many photographs confirm America's reaction to the news that their beloved leader had been so violently assassinated. Their horror, frozen in time, becomes palpable to me as I view the images taken on the day of people standing in the street, physically stunned. And I realize as never before the feelings of a nation united by grief as they sat riveted to their television sets. Not wanting to let their president go, they held on to every possible visual image as they struggled with the loss of what might have been.

ART: *William–Adolphe Bouguereau,*
The Holy Women at the Tomb of Christ, 1890.

Oil on canvas, dimensions unavailable.

Koninkiljk Museum voor Schone Kunsten, Antwerp Belgium.

WILLIAM-ADOLPHE BOUGUEREAU:
The Holy Women at the Tomb of Christ

As I think on this, my eyes are opened with new understanding for the disciples who visited the tomb early on Sunday morning. I love Bouguereau's painting of *The Holy Women and the Tomb of Christ*, and have found it a helpful tool to focus my thoughts while I attempt to read the story, with fresh eyes, found in the gospel of John.

> *...Mary Magdalene went to the tomb and saw that the stone had been removed from the entrance. So she came running to Simon Peter and the other disciple, the one Jesus loved, and said, "They have taken the Lord out of the tomb, and we don't know where they have put him!" So Peter and the other disciples started for the tomb. Both were running, but the other disciple outran Peter and reached the tomb first. He bent over and looked at the strips of linen lying there but did not go in. Then Simon Peter, who was behind him, arrived and went into the tomb.*[78]

Reading this as if it were a personal event, I can understand with my heart why the women would have wanted to return to tend to Jesus' broken body. Knowing they have seen perfect love face to face, I can sympathize with their need to be near him one last time. Lingering still, I become one of them and think, *A little while longer in preparation for the journey... a little while longer in his presence, soaking in the warmth of the sun....*

But then we arrive at the tomb and everything we thought we would find is altered. Everything we expected to see is gone... Jesus' precious body is missing!

See Mary Magdalene, in your mind's eye, as she rushes to find an explanation. Not sure what to think, she momentarily falters in her faith. Physically exhausted from lack of sleep, her mind is whirling with possibilities, and we are reminded of Jesus' mother Mary as she questioned the angel Gabriel. Our universal feelings now echo the theme inside our mind: *How can this be?* The mystery of Jesus' story is now folded over from beginning to end, and in this moment we experience the circle of wonder.

⁓❧⁓

Before we proceed to the music, I would like to reassure those of you who may feel unprepared for this kind of an artistic journey into one of the most sacred moments of Jesus' life. Fear not! There are no prescribed rules for retuning your heart to the feelings you might have if you'd actually experienced the Resurrection. These musical selections will lead your thoughts naturally into creating your own mental and emotional pictures. As you allow yourself to release the preconceived ideas you carry about these passages of scripture, the music will enliven your heart and connect your senses to the story. The only necessity for these musical devotions is that you allow yourself to relax any feelings that may pressure you, so you might be free to explore new emotional insights. I encourage you to find a way to quiet the noise in your life. Let go of your apprehensions and preconceived expectations so that you can enjoy communing with those women who first discovered the empty tomb.

DEVOTIONAL PRAYER

Dear Lord, we come to you now wanting to surrender our thoughts…

so we might immerse ourselves in the dawn of your Resurrection.

We admit that our attention even in the best of times is often scattered.

Help us to linger…

Draw us nearer so that we might begin to wonder…

Guide our hearts into these moments as we slowly breathe in…

Gathering with those who first peered into the mystery

of the empty tomb.

The Mystery (or Rosary) Sonatas
by Heinrich Ignaz Franz Biber

To magnify the tone of Mary Magdalene's thoughts in those first moments before the empty tomb we will consider one of the *Mystery* (or *Rosary) Sonatas* by Heinrich Ignaz Franz Biber (1644–1704). Each of the fifteen violin sonatas has a small copper engraving representing a scene from the life of Jesus or Mary affixed to their title page. These pieces distinguish themselves in violin literature, as they are highly virtuosic, requiring the player to use different "scordatura," calling for the tuning of the strings to be changed for each sonata. The recalibration of pitches changes the sound of the violin, giving the instrument an extraordinary range of sound. These special tunings allow the player to create previously non-resonant note combinations with a new vibrant beauty. The feeling of mystery in the opening of the story is underscored as we hear the violin produce sound transformed from the norm. As we listen and imagine Jesus' story expressed in sound, the four strings of the violin sing out with an unexpected quartet of voices, providing a fresh perspective that resonates through our soul. Biber confirms his intentions in his proud description of the work:

> *You will discover here my four-stringed lyre, tuned 15 special ways*
> *for the playing of divers sonatas... these I have elaborated*
> *with great care... I have consecrated everything that I have written*
> *here to the honour of the 15 sacred mysteries....*[79]

Even though Biber originally intended these sonatas for the private devotions of his patron, Prince-Archbishop Max Gandolph of Salzburg, it is easy to imagine the resonant opening chords of his "Resurrection" sonata being played in an immense cathedral, the new vibrant quality of the violin filling the hall, awakening our senses with a fresh, newly defined sound. Biber's message for a deeper understanding of the Resurrection lies even deeper: this music requires the player to cross the center strings inside the peg box at the top of the instrument, and again below the bridge where the strings connect into the tailpiece. Because of this, the symbol of the Cross becomes literally visible on the instrument in two places. In this way, the composer poignantly highlights the mystery of the Resurrection. It is as if he is telling us that we must see the suffering of the Cross before we can fully realize the glory of Christ's resurrection in the music of our lives.

Mystery (Rosary) Sonata No. 11 in G Major: The Resurrection, Heinrich Ignaz Franz von Biber

Rosenkrantz Sonaten (Mystery Sonatas),

violinist Sirkka-Liisa Kaakinen, Ondine 2014

As you listen to the opening chords of the violin, close your eyes and let the music awaken your senses to the start of a new day. You can feel the cool of the night slipping away as the sun slowly dawns over the horizon. Imagine the texture and sound of the dirt road under your feet as you walk with the women taking spices to the tomb in the early morning hours. When you reach the place where they laid Jesus, you notice the stone has been rolled away... rushing forward, you peer inside... your eyes need time to adjust... everything is so bright. And then you see the faces of angels and hear them as they ask, "Why do you look for the living among the dead?" (Luke 24:5, NIV).

You become frozen in this moment of confusion. Nothing makes rational sense. You try to find an explanation... you just are not sure what to think... all you know is that you must tell someone... and so you begin running. Surely Peter and John will know what has happened to Jesus.

Feeling the growing excitement, you allow yourself to hope. Maybe we can see the world in an entirely new light?

Rushing forward, you join with them as they gather in holy praise of the empty tomb, and without complete understanding you begin to believe in God's goodness once more.

Squinting into the light you sense a shift in your thinking—feeling unsure—retuning—then things unexpectedly click into place: We are bonded together in this moment of wonder, forming a new kind of community. Allowing ourselves to stand among them, we remember our faith is deeply rooted in mystery. Peering into the unknown fills us with wonder at a God who works quietly in miraculous way.

SHOUT HALLELUJAH!

I have seen the Lord! [80]

Suddenly our eyes are opened to the glorious nature of a day that will be filled with joy. This will not be a day for weeping; instead, it will be a day for whole-hearted celebration, as we have had official confirmation of the good news. The angels proclaim: "He is not here; he is risen!" [81]

Our hearts are quickened and beat with newfound joy for life. We walk with a fresh lightness in our step as we live the praise of the psalmist:

> *You turned my wailing into dancing; you removed my sackcloth*
> *and clothed me with joy, that my heart may sing to you and not*
> *be silent. O Lord my God, I will give you thanks forever.* [82]

Jesus is no longer lying in the tomb. Our God is victorious: he has conquered death. And we join with Mary Magdalene, the first to proclaim: "I have seen the Lord!" (John 20:18, NIV).

ringing the power of Mary's discovery to life requires music we can feel with our whole mind, body, and spirit. There is perhaps no other composer more capable of bringing us to the absolute peak of exuberance at the Resurrection than Johann Sebastian Bach (1685–1750), with his incredible Mass in B Minor. This music will simultaneously sweep us into jubilant dancing while lifting us up into the heavens with an overwhelming feeling of praise.

What began for Bach as a way to honor and impress his new sovereign Augustus III the Elector of Saxony, by writing a complete musical setting of the Mass, later in life became an ambitious attempt to showcase the entire height and breadth of his compositional style. And as if to perfectly express the heart of our faith, Bach places precisely at the mid-point of the Mass the singing of these words of the Credo:[83]

> *For our sake he was crucified under Pontius Pilate*
> *he suffered death and was buried,*
> *and rose again on the third day in accordance with the scriptures.*

To fully experience the glorious music of the Resurrection, it is important that we allow the mournful "Crucifixus" section of the Mass to set our hearts in place. Bach gradually quiets the music to further highlight the drama, as he leads us to slow down and fully breathe in the moment when the voices express *"and was buried"* one last time. To fully feel the moment of triumph, Bach's music will first poignantly descend into feelings of agonizing defeat; only just as the voices are drifting into silence, they very quietly, almost imperceptibly to our ear, shift from the dark feeling of E minor to the brighter tonality of D major. With this discreet reversal in tonality, Bach cleverly sets the stage for the surprise to come.

And suddenly, as if the music has been already flowing since before time began, a magnificent five-part chorus erupts out of the silence to greet us with joyful song. With the sounding of timpani and trumpets, we are startled into excitement as the voices jubilantly catch us off-guard. We can feel the laughter welling up inside us as Bach masterfully throws open a window of sound that carries us through a vortex into an alternate reality.

Mass in B Minor, BWV 232, J.S. Bach

Disc 2, Tracks 5 and 6: Credo: Crucifixus & Et Resurrexit,

John Eliot Gardiner, English Baroque Soloists and The Monteverdi Choir,

Deutsche Grammophon 2003

For me, Bach's story has become a guiding light, as I know he supported a very large family by quietly getting up every day to compose these breathtaking masterpieces. Even though he never achieved critical acclaim during his lifetime, he never ceased to give the world these musical windows into eternal glory. With his great Mass in B Minor, completed after he had gone blind and just a year before his death, he shares with us his true vision of God's amazing story. A lifetime of writing music illuminating the Christian faith now allows him to see, with his inner eyes, a glorious stairway to heaven. Through his music Bach tells us, "Life is filled with trials that tempt us to despair, but in this one thing I am confident: in the end, it will be victorious. Christ is Risen! Christ is Risen indeed!"

As I was thinking about the message of Bach's now-celebrated work, I decided to flip through the pages of my hymnal to find something with a similar feeling. Casting my eyes over the poetry I had sung for years, I was suddenly drawn in by words I had never noticed before in the third verse of "Higher Ground":

I want to live above the world,

Though Satan's darts at me are hurled;

For faith has caught the joyful sound,

The song of saints on higher ground. [84]

And I thought, *This is it!* This is how Bach's music creates a beautiful picture of our faith. With his Mass in B Minor, Bach is encouraging us to live on higher ground. Allowing his music to lift us up to dance with those who discovered the empty tomb renews our vision of God who is mighty to save (see Zephaniah 3:17), and able to conquer all things (see Philippians 4:13). We can celebrate Jesus' victorious return, and in this moment we become people freed from the debilitating power that fear of sin and death has over us. Hear Jesus' words now with new understanding:

I am the resurrection and the life. He who believes in

me will live, even though he dies; and whoever lives and

believes in me will never die. Do you believe this? [85]

When we experience the full glory of Christ's resurrection, we begin to confidently carry within our hearts the good news of our reconciliation to God. This then gives us hope that inspires a lightness of step, as we believe not only that we will see our loved ones who have died revitalized (see 1 Corinthians 15:52), but also one fine day, Jesus, face to face.

Listening to this music, our hearts become alive again with new hope of eternal life, and we understand the words of the Apostle Paul when he writes:

I want to know Christ and the power of his resurrection and the

fellowship of sharing in his sufferings, becoming like him in his death,

and so, somehow, to attain to the resurrection from the dead. [86]

God has turned our grief to joy because we have come to know a risen Lord!

NEW VISIONS

Come and see the place where he lay.[87]

How can we allow our new joyful involvement in the fellowship of the empty tomb transform our lives so that we might live as people of the Resurrection? To open ourselves to personal transformation, we will allow Gustav Mahler's *Resurrection* Symphony to carry us into new worlds of sound.

RECOMMENDED LISTENING:
Symphony no. 2 in C minor, Resurrection: Movement V (Im Tempo des Scherzos), Gustav Mahler

Like Beethoven and Berlioz before him, Mahler (1860–1911) takes the well-established genre of the symphony and fearlessly breaks all rules of convention to create an experience in music all his own. He does this in this stunning final movement, by calling for the "largest contingency of strings possible" and allowing the music to arrive at its crowning glory with a rapturous chorus.

While the themes of this symphony can be specifically projected onto the events surrounding Jesus' death, burial, and resurrection, late-Romantic Austrian composer Gustav Mahler intended his music to be understood more universally. Born in Bohemia as the son of a Jewish tavern owner, as an adult Mahler became fascinated with the themes of transcendence and renewal he found in other cultures, which eventually led him to his public conversion to Roman Catholicism. Because of the anti-Semitic undercurrents in Europe at the time, some have debated the sincerity of Mahler's shift to Christianity. However, rather than postulate on the dedication of his faith, it is perhaps more important to catch his futuristic vision of a time when there might be a perfect fusion of all faiths.

A lifetime of concert attendance, and yet I must confess I had never discovered this marvelous piece of music. Since this final movement carries themes of resurrection that gloriously develop over a period of approximately 35 minutes, I encourage you to set aside a special time when the house is empty so you might lie back and let this music wash over you. As you relax into this immense orchestral sound, Mahler's *Resurrection* Symphony will plunge your imagination into a full excursion of unknown worlds and cast a vision in your mind of a splendid new creation.

Symphony no. 2 in C minor, Resurrection, Gustav Mahler

Movement V: Im Tempo des Scherzos,

Zubin Mehta, Vienna Philharmonic Orchestra,

Decca 2000

The dramatic opening chords of this piece immediately throw us into a type of cinematic production of the mind. Mahler accomplishes this feeling by using a super-sized orchestra. In an instant we are made aware of otherworldly effects from eight to ten trumpets and horns playing offstage. Hearing them in the distance gives the music and the listener an opportunity to breathe. At various points throughout the piece, thunderous effects from the unprecedentedly large percussion section cause you to literally feel their presence in your bones; Mahler requires seven percussionists who alternately play eight timpani and a myriad of cymbals, gongs, bass drum, chimes, and bells. We can visualize the birds flying overhead as the woodwind sections (tripled their usual size) paint their picture, as the thick haze of sound is cleared away to open a path and prepare us for the story to come. Mahler gathers us around him to see a glorious rising, and we instinctively lean forward, knowing we are in for one terrific ride.

The orchestra calms and we hear exotic, bird-like calls from the solo flute. It is the song of a nightingale that magically harkens us into the world of dreams, casting its spell over the scene. We hear trumpets answer back in the distance, announcing a new arrival. The voices enter in a whisper, and we are carried away to an idyllic land where everything is light.

As you listen to this music, begin to associate the idea of light and pure energy drawing you heavenward. Hear Mahler's vision of perfection in these beautiful sounds. Allow yourself to begin painting your own mental pictures, and let these Spirit-led reflections lead you to write your own mysterious story.

For me, as I listen I begin to see a great conductor with outstretched arms directing a heavenly orchestra to hold the notes of a tension-filled chord. Looking again, I realize that I am among them. I turn to see that it is Jesus who is directing us as he encourages us to look for him in new ways. He masterfully draws each of us out of our comfort zone to create a new kind of sound. This will be music that holds the beauty of all creation. It is a fresh song of unity and reconciliation with God... and with humankind.

To find Christ, I must look for him deep within my heart, and as I continue with this music, the idea of this is so unfamiliar to me that I become fearful. Trusting, I begin to let go. Still unsure, I question: "How will I find my words? Who will be my comforter? Will I still recognize Jesus and hear his voice?" Slowly I explore further, allowing myself to feel uncomfortable, allowing myself to experience the pain of new birth. Watching Jesus' direction closely, I begin to anticipate the striking of the next chord. And as he turns me around to live again, facing the scars of my own cross, I begin to see the pain in the faces around me more clearly.

Suddenly the chorus is louder, more confident, as I see with new eyes the true meaning of these words:

For where two or three come together in my name, there am I with them. [88]

And the chord is struck; the power of his Resurrection resonating through me... through *us*... and I understand the dissonance in the harmonies like never before. And as I do, I find my place in God's music... hearing all the glorious voices for the first time.

> *O believe, my heart, o believe.*
> *Nothing to you is lost!*
> *Die shall I in order to live.*
> *Rise again, yes, rise again,*
> *Will you, my heart, in an instant!*
> *That for which you suffered,*
> *To God will it lead you!* [89]

Listening to this music of the resurrection enriches my faith, as it encourages me to linger until the thoughts of a risen Lord become powerfully real. Understanding with my heart that God was willing and able to overcome death strengthens my resolve to face my own darkness. As James Martin says in *Jesus: A Pilgrimage*, the sight of the empty tomb changes the meaning of the Crucifixion:

> *... where the world sees only a cross, the Christian*
> *sees the possibility of something else.* [90]

So if your heart has stopped beating with a passion for living, or if you are quietly thinking God has forgotten you... Jesus' Resurrection eloquently reminds you that your life can become vibrant and meaningful again. In this moment he readjusts our thinking so that we might continue to live in hope of a new rising. Yes! God is faithful! And may the power of this thought invigorate your days with the energy to see the possibilities all around you.

ART: *William-Adolphe Bouguereau,*
The Virgin of the Lilies, 1899.

Oil on canvas, dimensions unavailable. Private collection.

Image courtesy of the Art Renewal Center® www.artrenewal.org

"...there they will see me..."
(Matthew 28:10b)

French artist William-Adolphe Bouguereau (1825–1905) painted over 800 paintings during his lifetime. Popular during his career and widely accepted by Paris academic tradition, his paintings are filled with beautifully drawn women from classical literature and familiar Bible stories. Each subject is perfectly fashioned to express an artistic vision of women filled with sentimentality that becomes tangible as they realistically emerge on the canvas. Known to be a teacher of women artists, Bouguereau later became their advocate, using his influence to lobby for their admission into art institutions dominated by their male counterparts. As Jesus challenges the social norms of the time by appearing first to Mary Magdalene and allowing her to become the "apostle to the apostles," it seems right to feature Bouguereau's work in these reflections of the Resurrection.

By placing the Virgin Mary with the Christ child in a scene full of spring flowers, Bouguereau gives us a vision of Jesus being reborn, blessing us with his power and his presence. Having not yet made the personal connection between the Annunciation and the Resurrection, I had never associated the Virgin Mary with the Easter season. And yet it seems appropriate when we remind ourselves of God's original promise to Satan after his deception of Adam and Eve:

I will put enmity between you and the woman and between your offspring and hers; he will crush your head, and you will strike his heel.[91]

With the resurrection of Jesus, God brings these words into full bloom. With Christ returned to life, Satan is defeated, and in this way Mary has given birth to an entirely new creation. Edward Sri in *Walking with Mary* explains:

She is the new Eve, the woman whose long-awaited son will defeat the devil and fulfill the prophecy of Genesis.[92]

The white trumpet-shaped lily, commonly placed in depictions of the Annunciation to represent purity and virginal love, are now symbolically placed at the Resurrection, and these surprisingly hardy yet magnificent flowers become visual heralds announcing the good news.

REFLECT & JOURNAL

I encourage you to seek Jesus in new ways, with open eyes and an open heart to the world around you. Pause to consider how you might see Jesus' Resurrection every day all around you, and add these thoughts to your journal.

See him in the dawn that announces a fresh day full of possibilities as you rise. See Jesus born again in the hopes and dreams of others. See him as you notice someone stepping out of his or her comfort zone. Perhaps you will see Jesus in a struggling person who begins to walk with a new confidence in their step. Think of him when an elderly parent has renewed their strength and enjoys revived good health, or see him in a young student's eyes as they first shine with an enthusiasm for learning.

Yes, Jesus is resurrected every day, all around you, and his song of victory never ceases to give us cause for joy. As we continue to grow in our ability to see him every day, let us fill our hearts with this song of hope every day of the year.

The stone the builders rejected has become the capstone; the Lord has done this, and it is marvelous in our eyes. This is the day the Lord has made let us rejoice and be glad in it.[93]

For more paintings by William-Adolphe Bouguereau, search WikiArt for:
❖ *Song of the Angels (1881)*   ❖ *The Charity (1859)*

PART FOUR

SEEKING JESUS EVERY DAY

Come let us sing for joy to the Lord;

let us shout aloud to the

rock of our salvation.

Let us come before him

with thanksgiving and extol him

with music and song

(PSALM 95:1-2, NIV).

CHAPTER TEN

I AM THE BREAD OF LIFE

(JOHN 6:35)

Worship is a way of seeing the world in the light of God.

—ABRAHAM JOSHUA HESCHEL

PANIS ANGELICUS

May the bread of angels become bread for mankind;

The bread of heaven puts all foreshadowings to an end;

Oh, thing miraculous!

This body of God will nourish the poor, the servile, and the humble.

Thee God, three and one, we beseech;

Do us thou visit, as thee we worship.

By thy ways, lead us where we are heading,

To the light thou inhabitest. Amen

—THOMAS AQUINAS (1225—74)

FROM HIS HYMN "SACRIS SOLEMNIS"

We open our eyes; over 2,000 years have passed since Jesus' Resurrection. It seems that Jesus' glorious return has not happened as soon as those first disciples anticipated, and we have grown accustomed to carrying the weight of two millennia of discord in our Christian heritage. We can see that life is not a glorious symphony.

In our personal lives, there are bills to pay and the roof needs replacing, and no matter how hard you try to resist despairing, the world presses you to take off your rose-colored glasses. Changes at work cause you to feel the pinch of the economy, and you once again grow anxious about the everyday. As we examine the seasons of our lives, we feel them rolling over one another like the crashing of the waves. Time passes, and we find ourselves still asking: Was Jesus real? Did the Son of God really walk the earth?

Looking around, we see a myriad of church steeples that dot the landscape. As we drive past another church, we realize we have become separated, almost tribal, in our individual styles of worship. Who are all these people who have gathered behind yet another set of closed doors? And as we become faintly aware of our emptiness, we hunger for something more, and we wonder if our deepest needs can ever be filled.

How can we revive and sustain our feelings of glorious transfiguration? How can we nourish our faith so we might have the strength to journey through day-to-day life knowing a risen Savior? The answer is really quite simple, and the beauty of the mystery is breathtaking once realized. Our peace can be found by rededicating ourselves to the complete perfection of God's story. Our hearts quicken as we again remind ourselves of the richness in all the layers. By remembering how the pieces fit together around a table and a meal where Jesus is our bread, we know again that Jesus is the element that will unify our hearts. Without him, we merely coexist in separate segments, like broken pieces of glass longing to form a complete picture of God's spiritual feast.

Since founding God thru the Arts, I am continually looking for new art and music that will lead my heart towards a greater connection with God. I am always thrilled to discover a new treasure, as I know it will open my thoughts to greater depths of God's love and his abundant blessings in my life. In this way my spirit is fed and my love for God is renewed. It is "new every morning; great is [His] faithfulness... The Lord is my portion; therefore I will wait for him" (Lamentations 3:23–4, NIV).

Still fervently hoping for a greater intimacy with Jesus, I remain open to Spirit's leading. I feel the familiar ache as I once again look into the puzzling simplicity of these words:

> *Here I am! I stand at the door and knock.*
> *If anyone hears my voice and opens the door,*
> *I will come in and eat with him,*
> *and he with me.*[95]

Knowing my thirst for Jesus, various friends and relatives have suggested I might find the experience of traveling to Israel especially powerful. Surprisingly, however, the idea of walking in Jesus' footsteps has never held any attraction for me. Without realizing it, I had judged the need to stand in the same geographical space that Jesus had as sort of silly. These feelings of superiority had led me to unknowingly close myself off from something really quite special. I had become limited by my own narrowness. And so, whenever the idea of a trip to the Holy Land would be suggested in conversation, without questioning my motives, I would shrug off the idea and tell myself *that's not for me.*

But then last year, I was attracted to the title of James Martin's book *Jesus: A Pilgrimage.* Not realizing this would be a kind of Christian travelogue, I began reading as Martin journaled his thoughts and shared various insights as he experienced the Holy Land. His detailed description of the landscape and his openly genuine writing style worked together like a tonic to refresh my spirit. As he traveled among the familiar locations found in our Bible, Martin candidly expressed his moment of epiphany when first seeing the Sea of Galilee:

> *At that moment the Gospels felt more grounded,*
> *more tangible, more real than ever before.*
> *I looked out at the pale blue sea, barely able to believe*
> *what I was seeing... Jesus was here,*
> *I kept thinking, Jesus was here.* [96]

Reading these words, I became hooked. His excitement for the sights and sounds of this country became infectious. I could imagine myself riding along with him. As I eagerly turned each page and pored over every detail of his encounters, I became enthralled with the idea of traveling to this magical landscape.

In particular, I was curiously drawn to his description of the mosaic floors in The Church of the Multiplication of the Loaves and Fishes, in a place called Tabgha located on the northwestern shore of the Sea of Galilee, not far from Capernaum. This church marks the place where tradition celebrates Jesus' miraculous feeding of a great multitude. Primary to this sight is a rather large limestone rock protruding from the floor under the altar that is recognized as the actual location where Jesus prepared his inexplicable meal. And I thought, *How amazing... I have to see that!*

ART: *Byzantine mosaic of the*
Loaves and Fishes, c. A.D. 480.

Church of the Multiplication, Tabgha, Israel

Sifting through a wealth of images of the Church of the Multiplication, I discovered that the central mosaic placed directly in front of the altar nostalgically features a basket of loaves flanked by two fishes. This mosaic, the focal point of the church, pulled me into a world I had not yet discovered. The thought of several generations of Christians communing around this table exhilarated my cravings for deeper understanding once more, and I realized I had to dig deeper.

Identified as the earliest known example of Christian art in Israel, the mosaic has been preserved in the newer church complex, which was completed in 1939. Built on the site of two previous churches, this modern church has remained faithful to the fifth century style of architecture and therefore can be identified as a fine replica of early Byzantine decoration. Constantine's conversion to Christianity occurred in A.D. 335, and the schism between the Western Roman Catholic and the Eastern Orthodox Church in 395; this mosaic can serve as a window into the worship of Christians when our faith traditions were still in their infancy.

Art historian Thomas Mathews gives us a glimpse into the importance of these kinds of images to earlier Christian worship:

While the imagery of the ancient gods was largely discarded... a whole new language of imagery was developed to carry a new deeply Christian, world view. Christ was made the fulcrum on which all human history turned, and his body figured as the magic vehicle for transforming the lives of all his followers. [97]

He later describes the Byzantine aesthetics as a belief that the church "is the container for a religious experience" [98] and states that the location of the image that serves as a visual focal point moves the participant towards a deeper connection to the story of Christ.

Seeing the importance of Jesus' multiplication of the loaves and fishes to these early Christians inspired my thoughts towards greater devotion. I invite you to join me as I lead you on an imaginary journey; we will travel in our minds to experience this little gem of a church, perfectly placed on a hill overlooking the Sea of Galilee.

It has been a whirlwind of activity since you received the call from a friend to fill in for a last minute cancelation in their group tour to Israel. Not wanting to waste a spot on this once-in-a-lifetime pilgrimage, your friend wondered if you would like to join them on their church trip. Having no other reason than you have been looking for a way to fill your vacation, you hear yourself say yes. Thankfully your passport is up to date; but the process of closing down the house and alerting family to your change in schedule has been tiring, and you wonder what possessed you to volunteer for this long and arduous journey.

Because you have been added as an afterthought, your traveling companions are only distant acquaintances, and you feel ill at ease with them. Everything has been carefully prearranged; the itinerary is crowded, trying to take advantage of every minute of this ten-day excursion retracing the steps of Jesus. There has been no time to waste, and you have been jostled from one place to the next on a bus carrying people who still feel like strangers.

Tired, you descend from the bus in a haze and slowly tramp up the hill to another church so you might check it off your "must-see" list of tourist sights. Hungry and thirsty, all you can think of is your need for some sort of refreshment, and your eyes furtively search the landscape for the nearest equivalent to Starbucks. Amid the group you hear a buzz of conversation; someone cracks a joke about the heat; another person nervously laughs. You wonder how many more stops are left before you can return to the privacy of your hotel room and cool off with a bath before sliding between clean sheets for a much-needed night of sleep.

Feeling a familiar dull ache beginning behind your eyes, you follow the group inside the stone church. Immediately your senses are refreshed as you feel the drop in temperature upon entering. You blink, waiting for your eyes to adjust, and in this moment you take pleasure in the coolness of the air and the smell of the earthiness of the atmosphere. Instinctively, you feel that this stop will be distinctive in some way, and you long to spend extended time in this sanctuary on your own. A woman begins reading aloud from her guidebook:

"A Spanish pilgrim named Egeria, traveling in the year A.D 380, has written the earliest description of a church, memorializing Jesus' feeding of the five thousand. Upon viewing this site. she wrote the following description in a letter home to her Christian sisters:

*"Not far away from [Capernaum]
there are some stone steps where
the Lord stood. And in the same
place by the sea is a grassy field with
plenty of hay and many palm trees.
By them are seven springs, each
flowing strongly. And this is the
field where the Lord fed the people
with the five loaves and two fishes.
In fact the stone on which the Lord
placed the bread has now been made
into an altar."* [99]

Captivated by this description, and sensing the holiness of this space for the first time, you slowly move away from the group so that you might process things at your own pace. Amazing to think of this woman, who traveled a great distance to walk in Jesus' footsteps by the sea. There was no caution in her writing, no "supposed to be" or "traditionally believed to be" —just "this *is* the spot." Interesting to think of her standing in this very place, so long ago. There must have been many others like her, who were curious and wanted to experience a greater spirituality. This thought leads you to wonder about the community of Christians who regularly worshiped and welcomed guests to this region, as they were devoted to the preservation of Jesus' story.

You once again read over the information in your brochure:

*This church is a modern replica of the
fifth-century church, built in 1939
after the discovery of this holy site in
1889. The current church is built over
the foundation of two previous churches.
The second church, built in a.d. 480,
was an enlargement of the original
fourth-century church; the Byzantine
mosaic floors were added at this time.*

Gazing around the sanctuary again, you attempt to find the right words to describe this sacred setting that is creating a profound emotional effect on your senses. The space is really very simple. The walls are smooth and unadorned, and the colors are working on a type of monochromatic scale, requiring you to fine-tune your eyes to look for the beauty in new ways. The quiet and soothing nature of this environment makes you secretly wish you could live in a place such as this, and you wonder about a life lived by monks behind cloistered walls. The ordered days, the peaceful predictability, call to your heart, and encourage you to linger.

Looking down, you study the floor decorations and admire the plants and waterfowl you see represented there in a lush, abundant botanical garden. The scene is classified as the Egyptian style of "nilotic landscapes" made popular by the Romans, frequently used in mosaics of this period. These floors were chosen to represent a mixture of pre-Christian and Christian symbols of fertility associated with the mysterious life-giving force of the river. Since the name Tabgha means "a place of seven springs," this display of Audubon-like nature adorning a space that gently rolls in from the outdoors seems perfect. It fills your heart with admiration for those early Christians who designed and treasured this sacred space. You wonder what it would have been like to worship here in those earlier recorded years of our Christian faith.

Looking again, you make a closer observation of the colors in the tile work and their variation in hues. Black, tan, cream, various shades of brown and pink all work to suggest the natural tones of river stones one finds in nature.

Enjoying your solitude, you notice a crowd gathering around the altar. Not sure you want to intrude, but hungry to share the experience with others, you decide to join them around the table. Still unsure, you look down to see the central mosaic. There, placed before the altar, is the image of a basket of bread with two fishes on either side. Amazed, you hear someone gasp as the group suddenly realizes the meaning of the rock that bulges up out of the floor. "This is the rock where Jesus prepared his miraculous meal and fed the five thousand," a woman next to you whispers. Rather than finding a logical explanation for this tribute, the group decides to suspend their skepticism and read the story from the Bible:

When Jesus heard what had happened, he withdrew by boat privately to a solitary place. Hearing of this, the crowds followed him on foot from the towns. When Jesus landed and saw a large crowd, he had compassion on them and healed their sick. As evening approached, the disciples came to him and said, "This is a remote place and it is already getting late. Send the crowds away, so they can go to the villages to buy themselves some food." Jesus replied, "They do not need to go away. You give them something to eat." "We have here only five loaves of bread and two fishes," they answered. "Bring them here to me," he said. And he directed them to sit down on the grass. Taking the five loaves and two fish and looking up to the heaven,

he gave thanks and broke the loaves.
Then he gave them to his disciples, and
the disciples gave them to the people.
They all ate and were satisfied...[100]

Standing in this place, gazing at the location of this miracle, it becomes surreal to your mind; the story, heard since infancy, suddenly explodes from the page to life. *Jesus was here,* you think, and you suddenly feel the weight of several hundred years of worship in this place. Christians from the fourth and fifth centuries sat in this actual spot and unreservedly believed. They sat around this table and celebrated the Eucharist in the very spot where Jesus had fed the five thousand. Amazed at the magnitude of this, you wonder what partaking of the Lord's Supper at Jesus' abundant table would have been like in those first years after his Resurrection.

The sight of this place so lovingly preserved now fills you with visions of lying "beside still waters," and works like a tonic, restoring your soul. As you stand among these fellow believers, drinking in all the little details blended to bring the natural beauty of God's creation indoors, you *experience* real spiritual retreat; and as you do, you begin to imagine yourself flowing into a greater faith that all things are possible with God.

Stepping outside, you realize like never before that Jesus' story happened in this place. Looking out over the Sea of Galilee, you really see it for the first time, and you think, *This is where it all happened.* Jesus walked beside that sea and called his disciples. He walked on water and calmed the storm; Jesus was here, in this place. The church's connection to the surrounding countryside has allowed you to experience real pilgrimage for the first time. Looking around, you see there are others in your group, eyes still shining, who have also made a special connection to Jesus in this stunning space.

Allowing my mind to linger in a mental vision of this peaceful church, filled with mosaic floors preserved from an earlier time, pulled me in, and I felt the physical presence of this sanctuary urging me to delve deeper into my Christian genealogy. Unsure of what to expect, I hoped I might find a fuller place around God's table.

The placement of these five loaves and two fishes in front of the altar invited me to unearth the archeological layers of God's people. Seeing the tangible proof of the devotion of early Christians to Jesus' feeding of the five thousand, I began to sense how this divine meal had carried important overtones, harmonizing the familiar traditions of the Jewish people with the new vision of the Christian faith. To realize the deeper significance of the feeding miracle, and the profound effect it had on the Jewish people as they witnessed Jesus publically breaking and blessing the bread, is to begin to unravel the richness of Jesus' proclamation:

I am the bread of life. He who comes to me will never go hungry, and he who believes in me will never be thirsty... This is the bread that came down from heaven. Your forefathers ate manna and died, but he who feeds on this bread will live forever. [101]

For the Jewish people, partaking of these simple life-sustaining elements made an important connection to God's blessing. To see Jesus lift the food brought by a child to the heavens as he broke it and gave thanks reverberated with the message of God's divine providence that the Jewish people had regularly experienced during the eating of their Sabbath meal. It was therefore appropriate for the early Christians, of Jewish origin, to have celebrated God's presence around a common meal. Only now, as disciples of this new faith, they communed with God by taking in Jesus as their bread.

Having unknowingly stumbled into an undiscovered country, I became more curious about the customs of these people I had only read about in the pages of my Bible. As is usually my practice, I began my exploration of the Jewish culture by looking at the traditions highlighted in the ornamentation of several of their most celebrated houses of worship. Through this method I discovered a people who still feel very grounded in their faith by the practice of a living tradition carved out in the presence of God. From the comfort of my armchair I traveled from Israel to Toledo, Prague, Budapest, Liverpool, London, Paris, New York, and Philadelphia to view their most significant synagogues,[102] and I was filled with admiration for the heart of these people who worshiped God in such diverse locations throughout the world.

I was amazed to discover that since the destruction of the Temple in Jerusalem in A.D. 70 and their subsequent scattering throughout Europe, much of their spirituality has remained surprisingly intact. Despite the separation of distance and borders, the culture of the Jewish people has survived generations of persecution as a result of their regularly coming together to observe Shabbat. The marking of this sacred time begins at sunset on Friday evening, initiated around a table and the eating of a family meal. In this way they remember their roots, and they continue to ask God to bless their lives. Their identity therefore does not come from a sacred location, but instead from the regular observance of sacred time. As God rested on the seventh day after creating the world, the Jewish people rest on the Sabbath, and in this way they practice an imitation of God. This holy time, then, is when they commune with God's presence once a week.

To understand how these time-honored practices would resonate with someone raised in the Jewish faith, listen to how Susannah Heschel, professor of Jewish studies at Dartmouth College, eloquently explains her emotional connection to the moment when her father blessed and broke the bread of their Sabbath meal:

When my father raised his Kiddush cup on Friday evenings, closed his eyes, and chanted the prayer of sanctifying the wine, I always felt a rush of emotion.

As he chanted, with an old, sacred, family melody, he blessed the wine of the Sabbath with his prayer, and I also felt he was blessing my life and that of everyone at the table… and all of a sudden I felt transformed emotionally and physically.[103]

Her description opened my eyes to the significance of this holy meal of blessing, and how their weekly observance marked out the rhythm of their lives. Using these basic elements of bread and wine, they regularly sanctified or set apart a sacred time when God would dwell in their presence. I could see how they felt a mystical connection to their heritage that pulled them back through the events that branded them to God, the giver of life both human and divine (see Genesis 14:18).

Niggun of the Alter Rebbe

For those of you who are enjoying the added element of music for each chapter, I have selected the music of Richard Kaplan as he sings the traditional chant "Niggun of the Alter Rebbe." The music comes from a long-held tradition of calling the listener to transcend into the divine worlds of Creation, Formation, Causes, and Action, the four sacred pillars of the Tree of Life of the Kabbalah. These "vocables," or wordless text, hold a deep emotional connection to God for the Jewish people, and the spiritual feeling is universal.

Life of the Worlds:
Journey in Jewish Sacred Music

Track 13: "Niggun of the Alter Rebbe"

Richard Kaplan, Five Souls Music, 2003

Attempting to understand the multiplication of loaves and fishes in connection with the Jewish Sabbath can enrich our spiritual lives, as we join to a greater fellowship past, present, and future. We are whole once more as we celebrate God's creation and honor His care for the Israelites as they wandered in the desert. As we gather around this new Lord's Supper, we view Christ as our great high priest (see Hebrews 4:14), who is presiding over the feast celebrated in heaven as we surround the throne of God (see Revelation 19:9).

*V*iewing these events through the lens of the Sabbath meal, we will descend further into our story and linger among the Jewish people who were there the day Jesus fed the five thousand.

Imagine you have traveled by foot a great distance to see and hear this new teacher everyone is talking about. Following the crowd, you find yourself gathered along a grassy hillside, surrounded by strangers. Joined only by your mutual need to have some tangible proof of God's messenger, you quietly wait, hoping to see him perform some miracle with your own eyes.

Since the early days of your childhood you have heard the stories of God's divine providence. The regular retellings of how God rested after creating the world in only six days, the history of a nation springing from father Abraham's seed, a people who were providentially led by Moses through the desert to the "promised land" were your birthright. These were the stories highlighted each week as you observed the Sabbath.

You have always been mysteriously attracted to the recounting of God feeding his people with manna each morning of their forty years of wandering in the desert. The idea of this heavenly bread that was "white like coriander seed and tasted like wafers made with honey" (Exodus 16:31) has always called to you. Oh, how your heart cries out to personally understand, as David expressed: "Taste and see that the Lord is good" (Psalm 34:8), and "You prepare a table before me… my cup overflows" (Psalm 23:5).

Only these days, you feel as though God has forgotten his "chosen people." And you have begun to question the reality of these stories. Could God's extraordinary daily feeding have really happened? It has been so long since you have personally felt God's divine presence in your life, and because of this, the stories have become dreamlike in your mind. Even though your life has been richly blessed with home and family, you are still longing to witness divine action from God. As you wait in this place by the sea, you wonder, *How much longer must I wait?*

You have come to see this man called Jesus, who is said to be performing many miracles in the name of God among the people. Living in constant hope, you have traveled a great distance for personal conformation. Even though you are beginning to feel the energy of the crowd, you are tired; you can't really hear or see what is happening in the front. Rumors pass through the gathered people.

Some say they have heard he restored the sight of a blind man. A woman confirms her belief in his power with a story of her own healing. Daylight is fading, and you strain to see what is happening in the distance. Knowing you shouldn't linger in this remote place, you find that you just can't leave before you have seen one of these miracles with your own eyes.

Unsure of what to expect, you hear the direction being passed back through the crowd to sit down in the cool green grass in preparation for a meal. Wondering how such a large group of people will be satisfied, you decide to wait and see what will happen next. For the first time, you get a really good view of Jesus as he breaks a loaf of bread and lifts it heavenwards in the very familiar gesture of offering, thanksgiving, and blessing you regularly experience at the Sabbath meal. Instinctively, you know this will be special, and you prepare to witness this holy meal.

You have heard of a small offering brought by a child, and now you see this basket being passed among the crowd. Shaking your head in disbelief you are handed the basket of food. Seeing everyone around you peacefully eating, you suspend your skepticism. As you open the basket, you see *five loaves and two fish*, prepared just for you. Looking around you at the others who have already partaken of this miracle, you "take and eat," and you are miraculously filled.

Learning to lean into the moment of Jesus' feeding of the five thousand helps us to linger in the experience of God's abundant feast. We can now understand with our hearts how God calls us to live generously by faith, and we become practiced in seeing things differently. As we see Jesus lifting our individual offerings to God, he becomes our connection to divine blessing. We begin to realize that Jesus is how God will fill our separate hungers. He provides us with wisdom when we are thirsty for knowledge. He gives us community when we are longing for friendship. And his blood gracefully provides the sacrifice when we are hungry for God's forgiveness. With this miracle, Jesus sets the table and eloquently signals his ultimate place as the Lamb of God, miraculously feeding us with his presence. As he fills us, our over-whelming biological need for God's divine love is satisfied. Fully knowing our mutual need and seeing Jesus as our source of spiritual food brings us together. Making this connection to the "love feast," we gather to enjoy God's blessing of unity around our Lord's Table.

Communion is now different for me.

Seeing this mosaic in front of the altar, marking the spot of the feeding of the five thousand, has changed how I view our celebration of the Lord's Supper. I now see the connection to all the stories, and I am filled with love for all those who have worshipped in and preserved this place. I can now partake of the bread and the wine while remembering Jesus' sacrifice and how it ties us to the rich heritage of God's people. We are grounded,

not buried, in our heritage of the Sabbath, as we realize we are newly born children of the sunrise. We are rooted in a past that now sparks new growth from God's light.

And we are all welcome to sit at God's table. What a magnificent thought, when we realize the simplicity of coming with open hearts to offer our gifts to the Lord and ask for his blessing on our lives. And by the taking of these gifts, with this "bread of heaven" Jesus will spiritually nourish us with his very presence. Yes, Jesus is coming soon, and his return is ongoing. As we read the beloved John's account:

> Then the angel said to me, "Write this: Blessed are those who are invited to the wedding supper of the Lamb!" And he added, "These are the true words of God." [104]

DEVOTIONAL PRAYER

Dear Lord, we humbly bow our heads in prayer

as we realize like never before the shame of our grumbling.

We praise your holy name and compassionate heart

for hearing us when we cry. You are truly a loving Father,

who sends us excellent gifts to feed our individual hungers.

Thank you for the sweetness of your gifts, and

open our eyes to your wondrous blessings all around us.

Once you hook together all the meals recorded in the Bible you begin to see them as a vital part of God's story. Going further to look closely at all the accounts of Jesus teaching his disciples while sharing a common meal becomes powerful and central to our faith. The concept of the family meal is something so grounded and familiar to our common human experience that it is easy for us to immerse ourselves in these scenes, imagining ourselves sitting at the table among Jesus' disciples.

As I did this, I began to question why I had always thought of the meal on the night before he died as Jesus' "Last Supper." Since we believe in a risen Savior and since Jesus gathered around a table to eat with his disciples several more times after his resurrection, maybe I shouldn't label any meal as his "last"?

To highlight these thoughts and to prepare your heart for reflection on the image below, linger with these passages and reflect on their relation to our regular observance of the Lord's Supper. This will be a great opportunity to journal your thoughts as you honestly and prayerfully consider the following scriptures.

❖ *Jesus replied, "They do not need to go away. You give them something to eat... Bring them here to me...." (The feeding of the five thousand; Matthew 14:16, 18a, NIV)*

❖ *"Take it; this is my body." (Last Supper; Mark 14:22–6, NIV)*

❖ *Later Jesus appeared to the Eleven as they were eating.... (After the Resurrection; Mark 16:14a)*

❖ *When he was at the table with them, he took the bread, gave thanks, broke it and began to give it to them. Then their eyes were opened and they recognized him....* (Supper at Emmaus; Luke 24:30—1a, NIV)

❖ *And while they still did not believe it because of joy and amazement, he asked them, "Do you have anything here to eat?" They gave him a piece of broiled fish, and he took it and ate it in their presence.* (After the Resurrection; Luke 24:41—3, NIV)

❖ *When they landed they saw a fire of burning coals there with fish on it and some bread. Jesus said to them, "Bring some of the fish you have just caught"[...] Jesus said to them, "Come and have breakfast."* (The miraculous catch of fish; John 21: 9—10,13, NIV).

❖ *And surely I am with you always, to the very end of the age.* (The Great Commission; Matthew 28:20b, NIV)

ART: *Tiffany Glass and Decorating Co.,*
Christ and the Apostles, triptych window, circa 1890.

Leaded and enameled stained glass ,

side panels 80 ¾ x 34 ⅛ inches, middle panel 80 ¾ x 39 ⅛ inches.

Richard H. Driehaus Gallery of Stained Glass at the Navy Pier, Chicago IL.

While Louis Comfort Tiffany's (1848–1933) name and glasswork have become quite well known, it is surprising to learn that his unique style grew from an apparent lack of resources. It seems when he was yet to be well established, he was forced to use the glass from discarded remnants of old jelly jars. Tiffany discovered these materials, considered unsuitable by the more established glass artisans of his day, created an opalescent effect, allowing him the benefit of a greater range of color. Through these new variations of tones he was able to create a more expressive and lifelike language in glass. His carefully sculpted shading and highlighted flesh tones made his figures more three-dimensional, giving the viewer the impression they might spring to life and step into the room. Tiffany turned his passion and skill for glasswork to materials others considered inferior, and his innovational art is now highly prized around the world.

While contemplating Tiffany's amazing achievement, I began to see God in a new light. My heart could understand how he uses our imperfections to create a kingdom of infinite variety and possibilities. It is through our weaknesses that he shines the light of his love, refining our hard places as he molds us into a beautiful new creation.

Look closely now at the beauty of Louis Tiffany's stained glass window. Notice all the pictorial elements: the beauty of the garden; the presence of the table; the harmony Jesus brings to the circle. Imagine yourself worshipping in a sanctuary decorated with this gorgeous window. Close your eyes and feel yourself in this setting, engaging all your senses—what do you hear, what does the air feel like, what do you smell? Open your eyes and look around the room; it is filled with people from the past, present and future. You have all come to the table – a diverse community woven together only by your mutual desire for God's blessing. Do you notice anyone special in the crowd of believers?

Jesus is here in this place. And now, like never before, you see yourself eating a meal with him. Where are you sitting at the table? Can you imagine yourself, like John, leaning your head on his breast? Allow him to give you his bread—see yourself taking and eating it. Jesus passes you the cup, and you drink.

When we can see ourselves sitting with Jesus and eating at our Lord's Table, communion becomes an *experience*. And as we dedicate our lives to God, we eat and are filled by Jesus' presence as he nourishes our spirit—Jesus, our bread of heaven.

REFLECT & JOURNAL

Now that you have experienced the art of this chapter, imagine yourself once again among the first disciples as they take the bread and the cup with Jesus. Allow yourself to feel all the wonder of Jesus' words, "I am the bread of life"... "this is the bread that came down from heaven" (John 6:35, 58, NIV). As Jesus passes you the cup, what do you see? How does this scene illuminate your heart?

CHAPTER ELEVEN

I AM THE TRUE VINE

(JOHN 15:1)

Life is the flower for which love is the honey.

—VICTOR HUGO

JESUS, THE VERY THOUGHT OF THEE

Jesus, the very thought of Thee with sweetness fills the breast;

but sweeter far Thy face to see, and in Thy presence rest.

Nor voice can sing, nor heart can frame, nor can the memory find,

A sweeter sound than Thy blest Name, O Savior of mankind!

O hope of every contrite heart, O joy of all the meek,

To those who fall, how kind Thou art!

How good to those who seek!

O Jesus, light of all below, Thou fount of living fire,

Surpassing all the joys we know, and all we can desire.

O Jesus, Thou the beauty art of angel worlds above;

Thy Name is music to the heart,

Inflaming it with love.

—BERNARD OF CLAIRVAUX, TWELFTH CENTURY

TRANSLATED BY EDWARD CASWALL (1849)

*O*nce Jesus has spiritually filled us, how can we carry our awareness of him into our daily lives? How can we continue to see him blessing us with peace throughout the week?

As I enriched my prayer life by opening my imagination to see Jesus, I felt much more intimately connected to him. In this way He became more real for me and, through our closeness, my life source. I was not left out, but loved and treasured by the Son of God. I no longer felt the need to censor my thoughts in prayer; I could talk with Jesus and trust him with everything. Regularly seeing myself in the picture with him gave me the intimacy that I had always longed for, because while I was sharing my heart with Jesus, he *heard* me. And because he is God, he was able to love me perfectly.

Finally feeling secure in my place next to his heart, I realized that his love was unlimited. There would always be enough. And so, instead of feeling jealous or competitive with others, I began to understand that Jesus could perfectly love all those around me, too. Not only is Jesus "the Word, who was with God" and the "light shining in the darkness," but hidden between those glorious verses in the opening of John's Gospel was a message I had never really noticed before:

> *Through him all things were made; without him*
> *nothing was made that has been made. In him was*
> *life, and that life was the light of men.*[105]

However, seeing Jesus in the people and things around me did not come naturally for me. I needed to find a back-to-basics approach that regularly retuned my self-centered thoughts, so I could become even more open to seeing him in new ways in the world around me.

Twelfth-century Cistercian abbot Bernard of Clairvaux inspires our thoughts with his practical guidance towards an imitation of Christ that would ultimately create a "climate of heaven" within and around us. This excerpt, taken from an essay called "On Humility and Pride" written for his Cistercian[106] brothers, is timeless advice for us all.

If we are in Christ—that is, living with His attitudes in us—
we are quick to see the truth about our friends and neighbors.
We put ourselves in their place so that we can understand
what they feel and why they do the things they do.
We unite our spirits to theirs so closely that we understand
how their strengths and sins are like our own… We are happy
when someone succeeds because we are free from selfish
jealousy—or we may even choke with tears at their sorrows
because in compassion we feel their griefs as our own.[107]

And yet while Bernard's advice promised a pathway to deepening spirituality through a discipline of developing our eyes of compassion towards one another's common humanity, I found that seeing Jesus "in all things" meant seeing the Divine in people, too. This meant I must seek a greater balance of compassion for the humanity of others, while celebrating the miracle of the Divine all around me. Finding the equilibrium of this practice becomes our final step towards a greater awareness of Jesus in the everyday.

Contemporary author Ann Voskamp disciplined herself to creating a daily journal in which she counted God's graces. Through this process, she slowly opened to God's loving presence all around her. She directs us to see God's gifts in the smallest of life's pleasures: the feeling of warmth in your dishwater; the sounds of children playing; the sweetness of a crisp apple. We train ourselves to see God in all of these simple blessings, and as we do this we "whisper surprised thanks."

After a year of counting God's graces, Voskamp described an extraordinary moment while viewing Rembrandt's painting *The Supper at Emmaus*, when her heart was broken open to see the fullness of Christ in all creation. Because she had prepared her heart, she was ripe to receive God's loving touch. We become her fruit as she teaches us with these closing words how to see Jesus every day:

Counting his graces makes all moments into one holy kiss
of communion and communion comes in the common.
He will break bread and I will take and the world is His feast!
And He is love! and nothing will keep my hand from
filling with His.[108]

ART: *Pieter Bruegel (ca. 1525–1569),*
The Harvesters, 1565.

Oil on panel, 46.9 x 68.8 inches.

Metropolitan Museum of Art, New York City.

THE JOYFUL SOUND

PIETER BRUEGEL THE ELDER:
The Harvesters

Deeply encouraged by her thoughts and without having planned for the paintings in this final chapter, I became open to being led by Spirit. While I was still mulling over the idea of God's daily blessings, I found myself unexpectedly drawn to the pastoral world of Pieter Bruegel the Elder's *The Harvesters*. I was familiar with this artist's other works, such as *A Census in Bethlehem* and *The Netherlandish Proverbs*, but this painting was new to me. The idyllic beauty of nature paired with the simplicity of village life called to me. Wanting to fully understand my attraction to this scene, I felt the need to linger among these country folk a little while longer. Could Jesus be hidden somewhere within this painting? I had to find out.

Not knowing exactly where it would lead me, I decided to make *The Harvesters* a last-minute addition to our journey towards seeing Jesus anew.

REFLECT & JOURNAL

Before we travel into this scene, prepare your heart by lingering with this reading from scripture and my brief, directed prayer. Feel free to stop and journal your own thoughts before you read my greater description of the painting. I encourage you to continue my prayer by telling Jesus your own thoughts and concerns.

Like an apple tree among the trees of the forest is my lover among young men. I delight to sit in his shade, and his fruit is sweet to my taste. He has taken me to the banquet hall, and his banner over me is love.[109]

DEVOTIONAL PRAYER

Dear Lord, we carry such heavy burdens.

Each of us are trying to live up to some impossible standard,

and it seems as if someone keeps moving the goalpost.

We worry that we will not have the time and ability to fulfill

everyone's expectations; and yet, we secretly know

we must face our inner voice most of all.

Feeling like an imposter in a world traveling too fast,

we cry out for some relief from all the activity.

Help us to let go of all our concerns. Purify us once more

so that we might let your spirit fall fresh upon us.

ART: *Pieter Bruegel (ca. 1525–1569),*
The Harvesters, 1565.

Lower Left Detail of Men with Scythe.

Metropolitan Museum of Art, New York City.

As I first approached Bruegel's *The Harvesters*, I cast my eyes around the painting and began by asking myself: Where do I see myself in this scene? Who is it that I can personally understand? It didn't take me long to zero in on the man in the foreground, bent over and totally immersed in his work. His closed posture made me think I could understand him, working alone and completely unaware of all the activity around him.

Writing this, I realize the synchronicity of the moment: I am writing the eleventh chapter in the eleventh week of a semester at the college where I teach, and the eleventh month of the year is just beginning. I can feel the whirl of activity that always comes as the Christmas season presses down on me like an enormous wave, threatening to pull me under and crush me. In my present state of mind, I can relate to the seeming heaviness of this man's burden. The relentless nature of work seems endless. I can feel the pressure of the wheat enveloping him, and I wonder how much longer he must work before he can take a break and lie down under the tree with a cup of cool water. It has been a long, hot day, and now it is the eleventh hour, but still he cannot rest. He is alone.

I have known this heaviness of the solitary worker laboring under a load of cares. *If only I can complete a certain set of tasks, then I will be able to rest...* but the feeling of accomplishment never comes. Keeping my head down, I work on, knowing there will always be more, and worrying I will not be able to live up to all the demands on my time.

While I am troubled by my thoughts, something in the painting reminds me of a scene I have read in Tolstoy's *Anna Karenina*. He is one of my favorite writers; he can create word pictures of a bygone time that take you into another world. I could faintly remember reading a somewhat odd description of the "lord of the manor" mowing the tall grass on his land among his peasant workers. Sensing there might be an important connection to my understanding of Bruegel's celebrated painting, I became determined to find Tolstoy's account of this wealthy nobleman working among the harvesters. Although feeling as if I might be looking for a needle in a haystack, the book fell mysteriously open to the very passage I was seeking. In an instant I was pulled into another world, like Alice down the rabbit hole. I could feel the sun on my face and hear the scythes slice through the tall grass. "*The work was in full swing.*"

Levin, the protagonist, is suffering some sort of melancholy and decides to find his cure by passing the day among the people who live and work his land. He has tried his hand at mowing the tall grass of his lower fields before, and found the vigorous physical labor mysteriously therapeutic. On these other occasions, he had never mowed for more than a brief period. This time, as Levin takes his newly sharpened scythe from his foreman, he decides he will be working the entire day. Not sure if he will be physically able to keep the pace, he is still determined to make a good showing. Struggling after only a few short strokes Levin experiences overwhelming fatigue. Looking around, he admires the skill and ease of the workers surrounding him. The slow and steady pace of the elderly foreman, who despite his advanced age swings the scythe with ease, is awe-inspiring. Beginning again, he tries to imitate the flow of his movements. He slowly becomes unaware of himself; without realizing the precise moment when it happens, he finds his place in the work. Tolstoy gives us the accounting of Levin's discovery:

... though sweat streamed down his face and dripped from his nose, and his back was all wet as if soaked with water, he felt very good. He rejoiced especially knowing that he would hold out.... [T]he more often he felt those moments of oblivion during which it was no longer his arms that swung the scythe, but the scythe itself that lent the motion to his whole body, full of life and conscious of itself, and as if by magic, without a thought of it, the work got rightly and neatly done on its own. These were the most blissful moments. [110]

Tolstoy seems to be telling us there can be moments of sweet bliss in a sea of work. Instead of rising above our daily tasks, we can enjoy our labor if we learn to live in harmony with it and with those around us. And this thought, strangely appealing, gave me hope that one day my moment of transcendence would come, finding my place in the work of my community. My daily tasks would somehow seem lighter if I focused my thoughts on finding a balance between the human and divine, living and working within each of us. Instead of resisting others' visions or feeling the need to outdo their efforts, I flowed into their energy, allowed their work to inspire mine. I had to generously and compassionately love my neighbor while treasuring them as divinely made children of God.

Again, I reflected on the meaning of Jesus' words: *"I am the true vine, and my Father is the gardener."* And to magnify the importance of his words, he repeats this idea: *"I am the vine; you are the branches. If a man remains in me and I in him, he will bear much fruit apart from me you can do nothing"* (John 15:1, 5 NIV). And as I thought about finding a perfect balance of the human and divine in everyone around me, I suddenly realized—*This is Jesus!* He is our perfect communion with the human and divine. And because of my connection to him as my life source, my security, I am able to find his love in all things.

Standing back, I approach the painting once more. Seeing the picture as a whole, I wonder about the artist's intent; but more than that, I wonder why I have become so attracted to this world of harvest. Feeling overwhelmed at first, I struggle to find the right place to begin my journey. Considering all the options, my eyes continuously move around the canvas in a flowing movement. The panoramic richness of the golden wheat, the color of abundance, and warmth is calling to my heart, inviting me to step into this landscape.

Bruegel encourages us to travel into this scene by creating a realistic space with an immense middle ground that draws the eye towards the atmospheric haze of the distant harbor. Like hearing the gentle notes of a sweet lullaby, we are unconsciously pacified by the presence of numerous curved lines. The rounded corners, the hut-like bundles, and the curve of the scythe all illustrate this repeating visual motif, producing a feeling of restfulness deep within us. I decide to enter from the place closest, to join the little circle of peasants enjoying their food under the shade of a tall, lanky fruit tree.

Bruegel is known for his intelligent renderings of the Flemish commoner, and portrays a variety of personalities in this circle. As you examine their individuality—male and female, young and old—the circle becomes a symbol of the community, living in harmony side by side. One man leans over to slice himself another piece of bread; sitting next to him on the log, a woman holds her back straight and eats the perfectly placed cheese on her bread. You somehow know these people; they are pausing to rest from their work, each one mindfully eating their simple meal—feel the cool of the milk as it sloshes over the parched mouth of the young boy drinking from his bowl; the unquenchable thirst of the fellow who has upended his jug. As you enjoy these details, begin to imagine yourself involved in their simple pleasure of sitting after hard labor. You hear the gentle swishing of the scythes slicing through the tall wheat, and you are opened to the wonder of living close to the land.

Looking up in the distance through the trees, we can see the church steeple and just the impression of a home and garden, reminding us these villagers will eventually walk home to rest from their labor and worship together on Sunday. For now, we can chuckle at the detail of the man who has sprawled out under the tree for a nap with his pants unbuttoned.

Continue now to see the theme and variations in their work. There are women in the distance, some bent over tying up bundles of wheat, others gathering pears that have fallen to the ground. Lingering with them as they work, I imagine myself enjoying the breeze of the fresh autumn air as it blows across my back. Close to the richness of the earth I can smell the unique blend of cut wheat, wood smoke and fallen apples in my mind. I begin to think about a life that revolves around the seasons, and I wonder what it would be like to be so intimately involved with the production of my food.

The planting of tiny seeds in the rich dark soil that is always followed by the necessity of time; seeing the plants as they sprout and are daily nurtured into growth through the pure blessing of rain and sunlight. As you become aware of the energy all around, you find your place in the rhythm of the seasons and days. You feel that special contentment that comes with the knowledge of crops well harvested and carefully stored, appreciating the art of gathering in and preparation for the winter months ahead. You see the energy of all the different pursuits living side by side, like bees in a hive.

Continuing our exploration of the world inside this painting, we find the opening to the path through the wheat, and our eyes follow the women who are carrying bundles of wheat to some unseen location. The sound of the startled birds as they fly up from their hiding place causes us to look up from our work for a moment, and fill our lungs with the crisp autumn air. Scanning the horizon, we see the little hay wagon traveling the road below; following onward, we find the children playing in the meadow. Finally, our eyes come to rest on the boats in the harbor, thinking of sleepy afternoons and distant shores.

Stepping back, my eyes are once again drawn to the man working in the foreground, and I realize now that I had misunderstood.

This man was not bent down oppressed by a heavy load, but focused in sweet oblivion on the task at hand. Because he is unconcerned about those around him, he has become productively efficient. He has found the rhythm of his work because he feels God's energy of life all around him. And, knowing his place in the big picture of things, he savors the moment.

Breathing in, I relax and imagine myself flowing into the work alongside all the others. I am not alone.... Eventually finding my bliss, I think, *"Through him all things were made; without him nothing was made that has been made. In him was life, and that life was the light of men"* (John 1:3–4, NIV). In all these things—*Jesus is here.*

Looking back, there were times when I questioned God; times when I felt forgotten—left out—alone. I have stood off from others, doubting their motives, and, because of my competitive nature, found fellowship with them elusive.

It was only when I began to see Jesus all around me in the everyday that I began to understand his presence personally. When I stopped trying and really allowed myself to notice the small details, I could see that Jesus was in all things. He was in the warm embrace of my compassionate husband, and the cheerful call from a former student across the parking lot. I could sense his presence in the sounds of the piano drifting through the walls of my classroom, and in my youngest student sharing her newfound treasured library book with me... Jesus was in all these things. He was in the hope of new students, new friendships, and in each new insight... in all things, I began to celebrate Jesus.

Peace came for me as I opened myself to seeing the story of Jesus unfolding all around me. Doing this, I realized that certainly the beauty of his presence can sound like a mighty chorus, but it can also be the memory of a sweet girl who quietly sat next to me while I wept and handed me a tissue to wipe away my tears. Yes! The presence of Jesus can show up in surprising ways, once you allow yourself to notice... and really, it is more about our willingness to hear it as we travel through our day.

For more paintings by Pieter Bruegel the Elder. search in the Google Art Project:

❖ *A Census in Bethlehem (1566)*
❖ *The Netherlandish Proverbs (1559)*

Dona Nobis Pacem

his recording, featuring virtuoso cellist Yo-Yo Ma, is a fitting close to our meditations. He is considered to be an ambassador of world peace with his innovational Silk Road Ensemble, which regularly gathers musicians from around the world to collaborate on one stage. I admire him for his open and grace-filled work with other musicians around the world, and feel that his variations on this simple tune successfully encapsulate the feelings of peaceful, child-like innocence. I hope you enjoy them.

Songs of Joy and Peace

"Dona Nobis Pacem" variations,

cellist Yo-Yo Ma, Sony Classical, 2008

Not long ago, as I was returning home from a week of Bible lectures given by a great many scholarly and renowned speakers, I was deep in thought as I read through my notes, earnestly seeking the greatest gems of wisdom. Just as I was settling in for a quiet and meditative flight home, my thoughts were jarred loose by a child in the seat behind me as she began to kick my seat harder and harder. Feeling especially persecuted by this and wondering if the noise would ever subside, matters intensified instead as she broke out into full-throated song:

ROW ROW ROW YOUR BOAT GENTLY DOWN THE STREAM!

Oh no! Why me, Lord? I thought, *Why am I never allowed to enjoy your peace?* Then I caught myself—*Yes, I see,* and smiling, I realized that in this simple joy, *Jesus is here.*

Putting down my notebook, I turned to look out the window, and for the first time I saw the beauty of the landscape near my home. *My Garden of Eden,* I thought, and then I could hear Jesus speaking to my heart: *I am the true vine, and my Father is the gardener...* and I heard myself answer back:

Dona nobis pacem, my Lord—may you grant us peace!

DESCANT: *John August Swanson's Festival of Lights*

As our journey draws to a close, let the light of Jesus' presence grow within your heart. As we meditate on John August Swanson's *Festival of Lights,* see yourself joining the children of the world in this procession of peace.

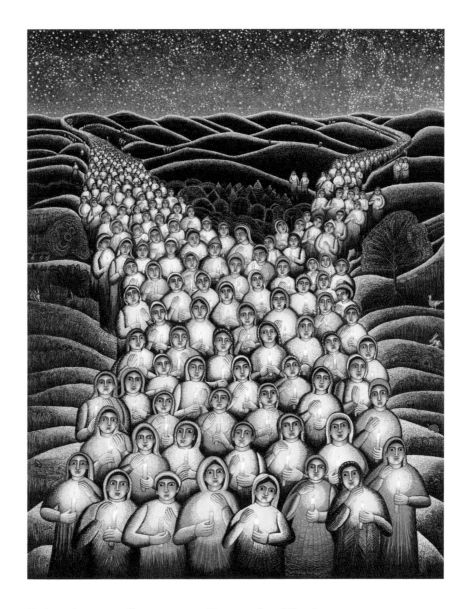

ART: *John August Swanson, Festival of Lights, 2000.*

Serigraph, 30.75 x 24 inches.

© 2000 www.JohnAugustSwanson.com.

Used by permission of the artist.

California artist John August Swanson carries us into a utopian reality with his lovely *Festival of Lights*. The peaceful consonance created through the repeated curved lines and circles is made manifest through his unique style, influenced by the colors of Latin American folk art and celebrated Mexican muralists such as Diego Rivera, José Clemente Orozco and David Alfaro Siqueiros. This serigraph, created from his original painting of 1991, is lavishly infused with colors that mysteriously glow. To achieve this effect in the printmaking process, Mr. Swanson drew a separate stencil for each of the forty-six colors used, creating a complex medium enriched with light. Inspired by a memory of walking in a procession for peace in Central America, Mr. Swanson describes the infinite beauty of the stars in the sky as "the symbol of candles shining in the dark night," and shares with us his vision of the children of the world coming together in a great procession of peace.

Gazing at this marvelous scene filled me with awe at the infinite variety of God's creation. I was encouraged by discovering yet another artist working daily in his studio to create paintings, highlighting his mission to "optimistically embrace life and one's spiritual transformation."

This thought led me onward to see how there are many others attempting to shine God's light into a world of darkness. I stopped to ask myself:

Have I been shining a light in concert with those around me? Have I been energized by their work? Have I really celebrated the beauty of God's creation in every person I encountered?

John August Swanson's painting seems to be the very essence of the familiar passage in Paul's letter to the Ephesians:

> *Make every effort to keep the unity of*
> *the Spirit through the bond of peace.*
> *There is one body and one Spirit— just*
> *as you were called to one hope when you*
> *were called— one Lord, one faith, one*
> *baptism; one God and Father of all, who*
> *is over all and through all and in all.* [111]

I felt the familiar yearning welling up inside me. With the music of "Dona Nobis Pacem" still resonating through me. I wrote the following meditation for Swanson's *Festival of Lights*. I hope you will join me as we are bonded together in our celebration of mutual peace.

Alone I begin—one spark

And I wonder if anyone will see.

Feeling the weight of the darkness pressing in, I falter.

Then remembering—"in him, all things were made."

Repeating this thought becomes the circle... the oxygen,

and the light within me grows stronger.

Turning now I see someone join me.

And his light is made manifold through our connection.

And now we are two and Jesus is here.

His fullness made known as we experience the mystery...

Fully human—fully divine...

And our two become four—and the light grows...

Lights now arriving from every shore.

A "climate of heaven" is born among us.

We see the wonder of the stars shining through the night,

their beauty all around us—His love infinite.

And we realize—Jesus is here.

Fully human, fully divine... Jesus is here.

A WORD AFTER

A NEW SONG

(JOHN 15:1)

Blessed are the people who know the joyful sound;
they walk, O Lord in the light of your countenance.

—PSALM 89:15, NKJ

HIGHER GROUND

I'm pressing on the upward way,

New heights I'm gaining every day;

Still praying as I'm onward bound,

"Lord, plant my feet on higher ground."

My heart has no desire to stay

Where doubts arise and fears dismay;

Though some may dwell where those abound,

My prayer, my aim, is higher ground.

I want to live above the world,

Though Satan's darts at me are hurled;

For faith has caught the joyful sound,

The song of saints on higher ground.

I want to scale the utmost height

And catch a gleam of glory bright;

But still I'll pray till heav'n I've found,

"Lord, plant my feet on higher ground."

Lord, lift me up and let me stand,

By faith, on Heaven's tableland,

A higher plane than I have found;

Lord, plant my feet on higher ground.

—JOHNSON OATMAN (1898)

Time and time again as I gazed at the stories of Jesus' life through these celebrated works, I would be taken back to the Sunday School classrooms of my childhood. As I meditated on each painting or piece of music, it would quickly harken me back to a gentler time, when Jesus was fresh and undiscovered for me. Experiencing each story anew, in my mind's eye, I could see the little girl listening to these events for the first time. As I embraced this memory, I felt the familiar ache to recapture her thirst for knowledge once more. *How had I lost her?* I wondered, and I longed to tap into the simple sweetness of her passion for Jesus.

Lingering there, I could conjure up several snapshot glimpses of times when I quietly observed my mother preparing to teach our Sunday morning Bible class. Meeting us in my memories again, we have arrived substantially early so that Mother might make last-minute preparations for the lesson. Together we are carefully cutting out figures for our flannel storyboard while Mother puzzles over directions created by someone with little regard for our lack of time and resources.

Frequently, after several minutes of careful consideration, she would exclaim: "Well, we're not doing that!"

Remembering this, I still chuckle as I am filled with admiration for her confidence in tossing out the suggested lesson plan in favor of making the story her own. She had a wonderful ability to bring these treasured stories to life with an enthusiastic reading followed by a time of simply encouraging our class into relaxed conversation while we colored the associated pictures. Her love of Jesus and her unique ability to personalize the gospel were her legacy to me, and the memory of these intimate times still continues to light my path as I journey onward.

These days, my mother and I enjoy discussing the Bible by phone; I can always count on the easy flow of our conversations starting as soon as I ring up to share my latest discovery with her. Led by the Spirit, these daily devotions have become a new kind of improvisation as we take turns sharing our thoughts and bouncing our ideas off one another. Always surprising, I can never anticipate the exact route of our discussions; in the morning I might hear of her fresh insight on a familiar passage of scripture or her discovery of a new book, while in the evening we might drift into singing a time-honored hymn just before we each toddle off to bed. She has been with me each step of this journey, and I am confident in her thirst for knowledge and her love for God—these gifts of her faith are endless.

Knowing Jesus' presence more fully, I look back on the road traveled through these great works of art. It has been several years since I began this ministry of God thru the Arts, and each new discovery has taken me one step deeper into my understanding of the love of God. What began like a sweet refrain reminding me of a distant melody that broke open the chains of bondage around my heart has now grown into a resounding chorus of a new song. Now I can see fully our God "has done marvelous things" (Psalm 98:6).

Jesus is no longer just a name I use to endorse my prayers, but a fully human presence that creates in me a picture of the Divine. The different episodes of his life become individual brush strokes creating a perfect picture of God. Connecting to Jesus' image, I can see a Father who has sent his love into the world so he might show us his goodness, and so that we might experience his presence *personally*. Knowing him as my Lord, I realize anew that Jesus is God's self-portrait—his symphony—his beautiful love song sung quietly within our hearts—and all the parts of Jesus' story make up the perfect pitch of the joyful sound.

Now I can see that each part of Jesus' song harmonizes beautifully with the others as the layers of his music are built up, one upon the other, so that they can uniquely resonate the theme of God's love throughout all the seasons of the year. No part is complete without the other, and every time we experience the story unfold, we grow in our devotion for God's matchless grace.

Hearing the fullness of God's music, I approach once more what is for me the time of preparation in the Advent season. Feeling his peace, I know that I will once again bow in wonder at the gift of the holy baby in the manger. Only this time, my celebration of Jesus' birth has developed into a glorious picture of God's divine nature, for I have stood firm in the presence of the Cross and danced before the empty tomb. The cycle continues—Jesus' story never-ending—and the song of God's love everlasting.

For faith has caught the joyful sound,
The song of saints on higher ground.

APPENDIX

GROUP REFLECTION
AND DISCUSSION

The following questions are intended for group discussion. Feel free to use them in any order, but for optimum benefit, I highly recommend you allow the class time to consider each of these questions ahead of time in preparation for your discussion together. Make a regular practice of introducing the questions and the artwork that will be covered in the next class, giving the participants time to reflect on their own over the course of the week before you come together again. Because of the wide variety of church traditions, please feel free to be creative by adding your own questions and scriptures to each lesson.

If you are working with teens, an approach I find really helpful is to have each individual journal their thoughts and responses, and then collect their journals. Young people are less likely to share openly in a classroom situation, but if you allow them to write to you, and then write a short thoughtful response to them in the journal, it can create a powerful bond between you, opening doors for your friendship to grow, as well as hook them on the idea of journaling. I use this method in my college class each semester, and I am amazed and charmed by how much my students are hungry to share with me.

Chapter One

Twelfth-century Benedictine Abbess Hildegard von Bingen is featured several times in the first chapter. She is considered the first woman composer in the Western European musical tradition. Having become a respected Christian mystic writer, she was given special papal permission to travel and preach to the clergy on themes of church reform during her time. Also a gifted artist and scientist, she was a pioneer of natural homeopathic remedies. I encourage you to use her music and art as a tool to focus your prayerful consideration of the following questions.

1. How did you picture God in your childhood? How has this picture changed or stayed the same over time? How do you picture God when you are praying?

2. Read the creation passages in Genesis 1 and 2. Take time to deeply imagine the Garden of Eden. How would you describe your vision of Paradise? (Just make a simple list of words.)

3. Examining your list, can you see something you are longing for in your current life?

4. What kinds of changes can you make to bring this picture of divine or sacred space into your daily life?

Chapter Two

1. As you continue to develop your picture of God this week, consider how you most often imagine him. What kinds of activities do you most often imagine him involved in? Would you describe him as distant or intimately involved in your day-to-day life?

2. Consider sharing your personal stories of a time when you remember God actively seeking you and drawing you to walk more closely in his presence.

3. Read the Annunciation passage in Luke 1: 26-38 and consider how Mary's greatest transformation came when she humbly accepted God's plan for her life. How does the story of Mary inspire us to desire and allow something to be done to us by God?

4. Discuss how you might allow God to live more fully within you so that he might transform your life.

Chapter Three

1. Consider the many stories in the Bible that beautifully illustrate the idea of waiting upon God's perfect timing. The children of Israel wandering in the desert for forty years; Joseph navigating through seven abundant years and seven lean years; the Jewish people waiting centuries for a Messiah; how do these stories color in your picture of God's nature?

2. There is an important period of silence and preparation in the story of Jesus. Allow the class to discuss and wonder about the life of Jesus before the start of his public ministry. What was his relationship like with Mary and Joseph? How did he fit into the family dynamic with his other siblings?

3. Light, Seed, Silence, Germination: Discuss this process in your own spiritual formation. How can you see the hand of God at work in your life in the past? In the present? Share personal stories of times you felt God was "silent," a time you felt your prayers were going unanswered. How was God stretching you?

4. Read Philippians 4:11–3 and discuss the meaning of Paul's secret. Return to the paintings in this chapter. In light of our study, what do you see? Which painting can you make personal?

Chapter Four

1. What are the kinds of things that cause us to experience personal storms in daily life? Can you remember a time when you felt out of control or overly stressed about a certain situation?

2. As you consider the painting of the storm by Rembrandt, to whom can you most relate among Jesus' disciples? Where would you imagine yourself into the scene?

3. In light of the events that will carry Jesus to the Cross, how do you feel towards these disciples as they struggle against the storm? What do you admire about these men? How will they change over time?

4. Read and consider Paul's letter to the Romans 8:36–9. How does Jesus connect us to the love of God?

Chapter Five

1. If you were to select one story as a favorite in the life of Christ, what would it be? Reflect on the individual personality traits you are connecting with in the story. What are you finding attractive about Jesus?

2. Make note of how you most often see Jesus in your mind's eye. How do you see Jesus when you pray? Where do you physically imagine yourself in relation to Jesus?

3. Consider Matthew 18:2–5 and reflect on the qualities of a child. Press into that thought and find a distinct memory from your childhood to share with the group. What kinds of activities do you remember enjoying with your family? What do you miss the most? How can we cultivate our "child-likeness"?

4. Return to the images in Chapter Five. What do you see? What attracts you to these ideas of Jesus? Do you have a story or memory of a person who showed openness to you when you were an outsider?

5. Read and discuss Paul's letter to the Galatians 5:1–6. As a group, share ideas how you can embrace your "freedom in Christ."

Chapter Six

1. Throughout his ministry, Jesus teaches us about himself with illustrative titles. Read and discuss the following passages as a group; share the effect on our relationship with him as we visualize him as the "the vine" (John 15:1), "the good shepherd" (John 10:11), "the gate" (John 10:8), the "bridegroom" (Luke 5:34–5), and the "true bread from heaven" (John 6:32).

2. Read John 13:1–5 and consider Ford Madox Brown's painting. Imagine yourself into the scene and ask yourself: What do you see? What do you hear? What do you feel?

3. To connect with Jesus more deeply, share with the group a time when you felt you were struggling to bond with a person or group you were leading. How did you handle your situation? What was your personal outcome?

4. Now consider this story from the disciple's point of view. How does allowing Jesus to serve you by cleansing you change your view of him? How can we regularly practice our acceptance of God's grace? How does this create in us the heart of a servant?

Chapter Seven

1. Since everyone has such a unique experience of the Cross, allow the group to spend time sharing their feelings about viewing Jesus' suffering. Consider discussing the frequency and timing of allowing yourself to dwell deeply on Jesus' pain and suffering during those hours on the Cross. What are some creative ways you have discovered over the years that bring the experience closer?

2. In light of our meditations of the Cross, read and consider Jesus' words as he attempts to prepare and comfort his disciples the night before he died in John 14:1–14. How are these words comforting to us in the present? What is Jesus' truth?

3. Consider all the voices you have experienced stretching across time in this chapter. How have you fellowshipped with these Christian artists? How does this encourage and strengthen you?

4. As time allows, consider the recommended painting of Durer's *Adoration of the Trinity* and Masaccio's *Holy Trinity*. How does seeing God's presence at the Cross in these paintings change your view of him?

Chapter Eight

1. Share among the group your individual practices of observing the time between Jesus' suffering on Good Friday and his Resurrection on Sunday morning. Do you have a traditional or personal practice that you find beneficial?

2. Read the account of Jesus' descent from the Cross and burial in the tomb found in John 19: 38–42. Consider Weyden's painting and share your impressions with the group. What do you see? Who or what captures your attention the most?

3. In light of this painting, read Ecclesiastes 3:1–8 and consider your connection to the words "To everything there is a season." How does experiencing Jesus' burial change your view of God? How does it change your view of your community?

4. Consider II Corinthians 4:10–1. What does Paul mean when he writes: "We always carry around in our bodies the death of Jesus"? Zero in and make this painting personal. How does grieving over darkness change us? How can we press into finding God's light in times of darkness? How can we see God's hand at work within our lives; our families; our community?

Chapter Nine

1. Share your individual memories of how you have celebrated Easter throughout your life. Do you have time-honored family traditions? Perhaps you have found meaning in a special scripture, poem, or hymn. How has it changed since your childhood, and how has it stayed the same? Consider sharing these with the group.

2. Read the story as it unfolds in John 20:1–6. How has experiencing the art and music of this chapter changed your reading of these verses? What did you see or hear that was new and surprising as you traveled through these reflections?

3. Using Paul's enthusiasm for deeper faith in I Corinthians 15:52, how can we endeavor to "retune our thoughts" so we might "shout hallelujah!" causing us to create "new visions?" Share with the group your feelings of victory in the past, and then together express your dreams for a new kind of future

4. Think of something you have become discouraged about. Have you stopped praying or lost hope over some situation? Consider returning to pray in this matter and ask yourself: "What kinds of things do I feel God might be asking me to release so that something new might spring into its place?" How can seeing Jesus help us realize more fully our personal resurrection? (see John 11:25–6)

Chapter Ten

1. Poll the group to find out if anyone has traveled to the Holy Lands. Encourage those who are willing to share their most memorable experiences. How did they feel before and after their trip? What was the most memorable take-away?

2. Encourage those who may not have traveled to the Holy Lands to connect to a memory of another place they have visited that they found to be sacred, inspiring, and full of the presence of God.

3. Read the story of the multiplication of the loaves and fishes found in Matthew 14:13-20 and encourage the group to fully experience, with all of their senses, the beauty of the church in Tabgha. Ask everyone to write down privately what they may have seen or discovered in this place, and then share aloud.

4. Going deeper into scripture, read 1 John 1:1–6 and notice how John stresses he has "seen," "heard," "touched," and "proclaimed" the gospel of Christ. Discuss his possible meaning, and consider how we might more fully share fellowship with the disciples by engaging our senses. What have you found surprising about these meditations? How have they provided spiritual food for your journey?

Chapter Eleven

1. Enjoy sharing your individual impressions of Pieter Bruegel the Elder's *The Harvesters*. Ask the group to consider: What is capturing your attention the most? What do you think this might say about your own life?

2. Paired with the painting, read and consider John 1:1–4. What are you noticing in this passage that is new for you? How might the Spirit be speaking to your heart through this passage?

3. Now consider Jesus as "the True Vine." Read John 15:1–5 and imagine yourself connecting more deeply to Jesus as your spiritual life source. Allow the class time to reflect on their own and then come together to share your individual thoughts.

4. How can we begin to see Jesus as the "human and divine" in those we come in contact with daily? How can we "shine a light in concert with others"?

ENDNOTES

1. Boyd, Gregory A. *Seeing is Believing: Experience Jesus through Imaginative Prayer.* (Grand Rapids, MI: Baker Books, 2004) p. 80

2. Genesis 2:8–10 and 15–17, NIV

3. Cachin, Francoise. *Gauguin: The Quest for Paradise.* (London, UK: Thames & Hudson, 1992) p. 170–1 [ce: fn 3]

4. Genesis 3:9, NIV

5. Genesis 3:21, NIV

6. Hazard, David (arranged and paraphrased). *You Set My Spirit Free: A 40-Day Journey in the Company of John of the Cross,* (Minneapolis MN: Bethany House, 1994) p. 24

7. 2 Corinthians 4:16, 18, NIV

8. John 1:1–4, 14, 18, NIV

9. Luke 1:26–8, NIV

10. Luke 1:30–2, NIV

11. Houselander, Caryll, *The Reed of God.* (Notre Dame, IN: Ave Maria Press, 2008) p. 18, 33

12. Luke 1:35, 37, NIV

13. Anderson, Lynn. *Talking Back to God: Speaking Your Heart To God Through the Psalms.* (Abilene, TX: Leafwood Publishers, 2010) p. 30

14. Isaiah 61:10–1, NIV

15. Matthew 5:14–6, NIV

16. Schneider, Norbert. *Jan Vermeer 1632–1675: Veiled Emotions.* (Köln: Taschen, 2007) p. 81

17. Luke 2:39–40, NIV

18. Lewis, C.S., *The Weight of Glory and Other Addresses.* (New York, NY: HarperOne, 2001) p. 30

19. Romans 8:15–6, 23, NIV

20. Hebrews 12:2, NIV

21. Gogh, Vincent van. *The Letters of Vincent van Gogh to His Brother, 1872–1886: with a memoir by his sister-in-law J. van Gogh-Bonger.* (New York: Houghton Mifflin, 1927)

22. Matthew 8:18, 22–7, NIV

23. Luke 9:23–4, NIV

24. Beck, Richard. "The Slavery of Death, Part I: 'He who does not fear death is outside the tyranny of the devil'." *Experimental Theology,* August 1, 2011. http://experimentaltheology.blogspot.com/2011/08/slavery-of-death-part-1-he-who-does-not.html

25. Romans 8:35–9, NIV

26. Mark 4:40, NIV

27. Matthew 11:28–30, NIV

28. Hazard, David (arranged and paraphrased). *I Promise You a Crown: A 40-Day Journey in the Company of Julian of Norwich.* (Minneapolis, MN: Bethany House, 1995) p. 92

29. Benner, Juliet. *Contemplative Vision: A Guide to Christian Art and Prayer.* (Downers Grove, IL: IVP Books, 2011) p. 47

30. Luke 10:38–42, NIV

31. Ephesians 3:20–1, NIV

32. Nouwen, Henri J.M. *Spiritual Directions: Wisdom for the Long Walk of Faith.* (New Your, NY: HarperOne, 2006) p. 116

33. Matthew 18:3–4, NIV

34. Weaver, Joanna. *Having a Mary Heart in a Martha World: Finding Intimacy with God in the Busyness of Life.* (Colorado Springs, CO: Waterbook Press, 2000) p. 80

35. Romans 8:14–5, NIV

36. Weaver, p. 211

37. 12 August 1963

38. Galatians 5:1, 6, NIV

39. Rundlett, Jennifer, "Christ the Redeemer." *God thru the Arts,* June 12, 2015, https://jrundlett.wordpress.com/1727

40. John 13:1–5, NIV

41. Smith, Alison. "Were the Pre-Raphaelites Britain's First Modern Artists?" *Tate Gallery Blog,* August 23 2012. http://www.tate.org.uk/context-comment/blogs/were-pre-raphaelites-britains-first-modern-artists

42. John 13:6–10a, NIV

43. John 13:12–7, NIV

44. Hazard, David (arranged and paraphrased). *A Day in Your Presence: A 40-Day Journey in the Company of Francis of Assisi.* (Minneapolis, MN: Bethany House, 1973). p. 19-20

45. McGuiggan, Jim. *The Dragon Slayer: Reflections on the Saving of the World.* (McGuiggan Publishing, 2004) p.78

46. Ibid. p. 178

47. http://fineartamerica.com/featured/crucifixion-jodie-marie-anne-richardson-traugott---aka-jm-art-.html. Photographed in Santa Fe, NM, Cathedral Basilica of Saint Francis of Assisi. Used by permission of the artist.

48. Personal correspondence between the author and the artist, June 9, 2015

49. Ibid.

50. Flood, Derek, *Healing the Gospel: A Radical Vision for Grace, Justice and the Cross,* (Wipf & Stock, 2012) p. 42

51. Luke 23:34, NIV

52. Luke 23:41–2, NIV

53. Luke 23:43, NIV

54. Taken from the *Good Friday Versicle* of the Roman Catholic stational liturgy commonly used for the Veneration of the Cross on Good Friday. http://jfrankhenderson.com/pdf/goodfridayveneration.pdf

55. John 19:26–7

56. Mark 15:34, NIV

57. John 19:28, NIV

58. Taken from the *Good Friday Reproaches*

59. John 19:30, NIV

60. Luke 23:46, NIV

61. Matthew 7: 24–5, NIV

62. Revelations 5:6a, 7, NIV

63. John 12:24, NIV

64. John 12:36, NIV

65. Houselander, Caryll. *The Way of the Cross.* (Liguori, MO: Liguori Publications, 2002) p. 110

66. Ibid. p.109

67. *The Student Bible Notes,* NIV. Philip Yancey and Tim Stafford. (Grand Rapids MI: Zondervan,1996) p. 1299

68. Burke, Daniel. "What Did Jesus Do on Holy Saturday" in *The Washington Post*, April 3, 2012. http://www.washingtonpost.com/national/on-faith/what-did-jesus-do-on-holy-saturday/2012/04/02/gIQATLMSrS_story.html

69. Alfeyev, Bishop Hilarion. "Christ the Conqueror of Hell." Department for External Church Relations of the Moscow Patriarchate, May 21, 2013. Reprinted from "The Descent of Christ into Hades in Eastern and Western Theological Traditions" lecture (given at St. Mary's Cathedral, Minneapolis, November 5, 2002). *http://orthodoxeurope.org/print/11/1/5.aspx*

70. John 19:38–42, NIV

71. John 3:21, NIV

72. à Kempis, Thomas. *On the Passion of Christ According to the Four Evangelist,* trans. J. N. Tylenda. (San Francisco, CA: Ignatius Press, 2004) p. 152

73. Altrock, Chris. *Prayers from the Pit: Praying in Times of Pain.* (Nashville TN: 21st Century Christian, 2010) p. 99

74. 2 Corinthians 4:10–1, NIV

75. John 20:1, NIV

76. Wright, N.T. *Scripture and the Authority of God.* (New York, NY: HarperCollins, 2011) p. 25

77. Seamands, David A. *Healing for Damaged Emotions* (Wheaton, IL: Victor Books, 1991) p. 12

78. John 20:1–6a, NIV

79. *Dedication to Archbishop Max Gandolph, Denkmäler der Tonkunst in Österreich series.* 1898. Quoted in the liner notes by Reinhard Goebel (trans. Michael Talbot), Archiv Production, Deutsche Grammophon, 1991.

80. John 20:18, NIV

81. Luke 24:6, NIV

82. Psalm 30:11–2, NIV

83. Words from the Niceno-Constantinopolitan Creed written in A.D. 325 by early church fathers of the ecumenical First and Second Councils that met in Nicea. The Nicene Creed is still widely used as an expression of the major tenets of the Christian faith.

84. "Higher Ground" by Johnston Oatman, 1898

85. John 11:25–6, NIV

86. Philippians 3:10–1, NIV

87. Matthew 28:6, NIV

88. Matthew 18:20, NIV

89. *Die Auferstehung*, F.G. Klopstock. Text altered by Gustav Mahler for Symphony no. 2, the *Resurrection*.

90. Martin, James. *Jesus: A Pilgrimage* (New York, NY: HarperOne, 2014) p. 414

91. Genesis 3:15, NIV

92. Sri, Edward. *Walking with Mary: A Biblical Journey from Nazareth to the Cross.* (New York, NY: Image, 2013) p. 127

93. Psalm 118:22–4, NIV

94. Note: The difference in expression and size of each side of Christ's face is intentional, as the icon is expressing Christ's nature as larger than life, simultaneously fully human and fully divine. "The object is not to create a realistic impression…it is to lead the thoughts towards an existence that is 'without end'." Solrunn Nes, *The Mystical Language of Icons.* William B. Eerdmans, Grand Rapids, MI/Cambridge, U.K. (p.20)

95. Revelations 3:20, NIV

96. Martin, James. *Jesus: A Pilgrimage.* (New York, NY: HarperOne, 2014) p. 30–1

97. Matthews, Thomas. *Byzantium: From Antiquity to the Renaissance.* (New Haven, CT: Yale University Press, 1998) p. 15

98. Ibid. p. 97

99. Murphy-O'Connor, Jerome. *The Holy Lands: An Oxford Archeological Guide from the Earliest times to 1700.* (Oxford University Press, 1998) page unknown

100. Matthew 14:13–20a, NIV

101. John 6:35, 58, NIV

102. *Art of Faith: Judaism–Christianity–Islam, The Architecture and Art of the Most Significant Religious Buildings of the World.* Alive/Mind DVD series. (New York, NY: Illuminations Television, 2008)

103. Heschel, Susannah. Introduction to *The Sabbath* by Abraham Joshua Heschel.(FSG Classics, 2005)

104. Revelations 19:9, NIV

105. John 1:3–4, NIV

106. It is interesting to note that the Cistercian brotherhood lived in the constant rhythm of prayer, contemplation, study, worship, and manual labor, mainly working in the fields.

107. Hazard, David (arranged and paraphrased). *Your Angels Guard My Steps: A 40-Day Journey in the Company of Bernard of Clairvaux.* (Minneapolis, MN: Bethany House, 1998) p. 101

108. Voskamp, Ann. *One Thousand Gifts: Dare to Live Fully Right Where You Are.* (Grand Rapids, MI: Zondervan, 2010) p. 221

109. Song of Songs 2:3–4, NIV

110. Tolstoy, Leo. *Anna Karenina*, trans. Richard Pevear & Larissa Volokhonsky. (Penguin Classics Deluxe Edition, 2000) p. 252

111. Ephesians 4:3–6, NIV

BIBLIOGRAPHY

All Scriptures used taken from *The Student Bible*, New International Version. Grand Rapids, MI: Zondervan, 1996.

à Kempis, Thomas. *On the Passion of Christ According to the Four Evangelists*, trans. J.N. Tylenda. San Francisco, CA: Ignatius Press, 2004.

Alfeyev, Bishop Hilarion. "Christ the Conqueror of Hell." Department for External Church Relations of the Moscow Patriarchate, May 21, 2013. Reprinted from "The Descent of Christ into Hades in Eastern and Western Theological Traditions" lecture (given at St. Mary's Cathedral, Minneapolis, November 5, 2002). http://orthodoxeurope.org/print/11/1/5.aspx

Altrock, Chris. *Prayers from the Pit: Praying in Times of Pain*. Nashville, TN: 21st Century Christian, 2010.

Anderson, Lynn. *Talking Back to God: Speaking Your Heart to God Through the Psalms*. Abilene, TX: Leafwood Publishers, 2010.

Art of Faith: Judaism–Christianity–Islam, The Architecture and Art of the Most Significant Religious Buildings of the World. Alive/Mind DVD series. New York: Illuminations Television, 2008.

Beck, Richard. "The Slavery of Death, Part I: 'He who does not fear death is outside the tyranny of the devil'." *Experimental Theology*, August 1, 2011. http://experimentaltheology.blogspot.com/2011/08/slavery-of-death-part-1-he-who-does-not.html

Benner, Juliet. *Contemplative Vision: A Guide to Christian Art and Prayer*. Downers Grove, IL: IVP Books, 2011.

Bockemühl, Michael. *Rembrandt 1606–1669: The Mystery of the Revealed Form*. Köln: Taschen, 2007.

Boyd, Gregory A. *Seeing is Believing: Experience Jesus through Imaginative Prayer*. Grand Rapids, MI: Baker Books, 2004.

Burke, Daniel. "What Did Jesus do on Holy Saturday." *The Washington Post*, April 3, 2012. http://www.washingtonpost.com/national/on-faith/what-did-jesus-do-on-holy-saturday/2012/04/02/gIQATLMSrS_story.html

Butts, K. Rex. "Easter's Promise for the Broken Heart." *Peter's Patter: Facilitation Spiritual Conversations*, March 30, 2013. https://ozziepete.wordpress.com/2013/03/30/easters-promise-for-the-broken-heart/

Cachin, Françoise. *Gauguin: The Quest for Paradise*. London, UK: Thames & Hudson, 1992.

Carr, Allen. "Being People of Resurrection." *Sacred Margins*, April 16, 2014. http://sacredmargins.com/2014/04/16/being-people-of-resurrection/

Davis, Dr. C. Truman. "A Physician's View of the Crucifixion of Jesus Christ." *The Christian Broadcasting Network*, no date given. http://www.cbn.com/spirituallife/onlinediscipleship/easter/a_physician's_view_of_the_crucifixion_of_jesus_christ.aspx

Dobbs, John. "What Question Does the Resurrection Answer?" *Out Here Hope Remains*, February 5, 2012. http://johndobbs.com/what-question-does-the-resurrection-answer/ - comment-61995

Emmerich, Anne Catherine. *The Dolorous Passion of Our Lord Jesus Christ*. Reproduction of the twenty-fourth edition by Burns, Oates & Washbourne Ltd., London, 1923. Mineola, NY: Dover, 2004.

Flood, Derek. *Healing the Gospel: A Radical vision for Grace, Justice and the Cross*. Wipf & Stock Pub, 2012.

Gogh, Vincent van. *The Letters of Vincent van Gogh to His Brother, 1872—1886: with a memoir by his sister-in-law J. van Gogh-Bonger*. New York: Houghton Mifflin, 1927.

Heschel, Susannah. Introduction to *The Sabbath* by Abraham Joshua Heschel. FSG Classics, 2005.

Hahn, Scott. *The Lamb's Supper: The Mass as Heaven on Earth*. New York, NY: Doubleday, 1999.

Horne, Peter. "Sunday Isn't Friday." *Peter's Patter: Facilitating Spiritual Conversations*, April 24, 2014. https://ozziepete.wordpress.com/2014/04/24/sunday-isnt-friday/

Hazard, David (arranged and paraphrased). *You Set My Spirit Free: A 40-Day Journey in the Company of John of the Cross*. Minneapolis, MN: Bethany House, 1994.

Hazard, David (arranged and paraphrased). *I Promise You a Crown: A 40-Day Journey in the Company of Julian of Norwich*. Minneapolis, MN: Bethany House, 1995.

Hazard, David (arranged and paraphrased). *A Day in Your Presence: A 40-Day Journey in the Company of Francis of Assisi*. Minneapolis, MN: Bethany House, 1973.

Hazard, David (arranged and paraphrased). *Your Angels Guard My Steps; A 40-Day Journey in the Company of Bernard of Clairvaux*. Minneapolis, MN: Bethany House, 1998.

Houselander, Caryll. *The Reed of God.* Notre Dame, IN: Ave Maria Press, 2008.

Houselander, Caryll. *The Way of the Cross.* Liguori , MO: Liguori Publications, 2002.

Kavanaugh, Patrick. *Spiritual Lives of the Great Composers*, revised and expanded edition. Grand Rapids, MI: Zondervan, 1996.

Klugewicz, Stephen. "Ten Classical Music Pieces for Easter." *The Imaginative Conservative*, April 4, 2015. http://www.theimaginativeconservative.org/2015/04/ten-classical-music-pieces-for-easter.html

Lewis, C.S., *The Weight of Glory and Other Addresses.* New York, NY: HarperOne, 2001.

Martin, James. *Jesus: A Pilgrimage.* New York, NY: HarperOne, 2014.

Matthews, Thomas. *Byzantium: From Antiquity to the Renaissance.* New Haven, CT: Yale University Press, 1998.

McGuiggan, Jim. *The Dragon Slayer: Reflections on the Saving of the World.* McGuiggan Publishing, 2004.

Mooney, Tim. "Praying with Art—Visio Divina." *Patheos: Hosting the Conversation of Faith*, July 13, 2009. http://www.patheos.com/Resources/Additional-Resources/Praying-with-Art-Visio-Divina

Murphy-O'Connor, Jerome. *The Holy Lands: An Oxford Archeological Guide from the Earliest Times to 1700.* Fourth edition. Oxford, UK: Oxford University Press, 1998.

Nes, Solrunn. *The Mystical Language of Icons.* Grand Rapids, MI: William B. Eerdmans, 2005.

Nouwen, Henri J.M. *Spiritual Directions: Wisdom for the Long Walk of Faith.* New York, NY: HarperOne, 2006.

Rundlett, Jennifer. *My Dancing Day: Reflections of the Incarnation in Art and Music.* Frederick, MD: God thru the Arts, 2013.

Saunders, Rev. William. "The Symbolism of the Pelican." CERC, reprinted with permission from Arlington Catholic Herald, 2003. http://www.catholiceducation.org/en/culture/catholic-contributions/the-symbolism-of-the-pelican.html

Schneider, Norbert. *Jan Vermeer 1632–1675: Veiled Emotions.* Köln: Taschen, 2007.

Seamands, David A. *Healing for Damaged Emotions.* Wheaton, IL: Victor Books, 1991.

Smith, Alison. "Were the Pre-Raphaelites Britain's First Modern Artists?" *Tate Gallery Blog*, August 23, 2012. http://www.tate.org.uk/context-comment/blogs/were-pre-raphaelites-britains-first-modern-artists,

Sri, Edward, *Walking with Mary: A Biblical Journey from Nazareth to the Cross.* New York, NY: Image, 2013.

"The Timeline of the John F. Kennedy Assassination," Wikipedia, last modified 24 February 2016. https://en.wikipedia.org/wiki/Timeline_of_the_John_F._Kennedy_assassination#CITEREFAssociated_Press1963

Tolstoy, Leo. *Anna Karenina*, trans Richard Pevear & Larissa Volokhonsky. Penguin Classics Deluxe Edition, 2000.

Voskamp, Ann. *One Thousand Gifts: Dare to Live Fully Right Where You Are.* Grand Rapids MI: Zondervan, 2010.

Walther, Ingo F. *Paul Gauguin, 1848–1903: The Primitive Sophisticate.* Köln: Taschen, 1999.

Weaver, Joanna. *Having a Mary Heart in a Martha World: Finding Intimacy with God in the Busyness of Life.* Colorado Springs, CO: Waterbook Press, 2000.

Williams, Matt. "A Universe of 10 Dimensions." *Universe Today: Space and Astronomy News*, December 10, 2014. http://www.universetoday.com/48619/a-universe-of-10-dimensions/

Wisse, Jacob. "Pieter Bruegel the Elder (c. 1525–1569)". *Heilbrunn Timeline of Art History*. New York: The Metropolitan Museum of Art, 2000–. http://www.metmuseum.org/toah/hd/brue/hd_brue.htm (October 2002)

Wright, N.T. *Scripture and the Authority of God.* New York, NY: HarperCollins, 2011.

Zuffi, Stefano. *Gospel Figures In Art. Translated by Thomas Michael Hartmann.* Los Angeles, CA: J. Paul Getty Museum, 2003.

Yancey, Philip and Tim Stafford. *The Student Bible Notes,* NIV. Grand Rapids MI: Zondervan, 1996.

ART CITATIONS

(Pg. 14) Hildegard von Bingen, *The Choirs of Angels*. 1151–2. Scivias 1.6. Rubertsberg Manuscript, fol. 38r. Public domain. Source: https://commons.wikimedia.org/wiki/File:07angels-hildegard_von_bingen.jpg

(Pg. 23) Paul Gauguin, *Frauen und Schimmel*, 1903. Oil on canvas, 28 ½ x 36 inches. Museum of Fine Arts, Boston. Public domain. Source: https://commons.wikimedia.org/wiki/File:Paul_Gauguin_057.jpg#.7B.7Bint:license-header.7D.7D

(Pg. 31) Paul Gauguin, *Caricature Self-Portrait*, 1889. Oil on wood, 31 3/16 x 20 3/16 inches. Chester Dale Collection, National Gallery of Art, Washington DC. Public domain. Source: NGA Open Access

(Pg. 43) Henry Ossawa Tanner, *Annunciation*, 1898. Oil on canvas, 57 x 71 ¼ inches. Philadelphia Museum of Art. Public domain. Source: https://commons.wikimedia.org/wiki/File:Henry_Ossawa_Tanner_-_The_Annunciation.jpg

(Pg. 50) Henry Ossawa Tanner, *The Banjo Lesson,* 1893. Oil on canvas, 49 x 35 ½ inches. Hampton University Museum, Hampton, Virginia. Public domain. Source: https://commons.wikimedia.org/wiki/File:Henry_Ossawa_Tanner_-_The_Banjo_Lesson.jpg

(Pg. 60) Johannes Vermeer, *The Allegory of Faith,* c. 1670–72. Oil on canvas, 45 x 35 inches. Friedsam Collection, Metropolitan Museum of Art, New York. This image is part of the Met's OASC (Open Access for Scholarly Content) collection. Source: http://www.metmuseum.org/collection/the-collection-online/search/437877

(Pg.63) Johannes Vermeer, *Woman Holding a Balance*, 1664. Oil on canvas, 15 5/8 x 14 inches. Widener Collection, National Gallery of Art, Washington DC. Public domain. Source: NGA Open Access

(Pg. 74) Rembrandt van Rijn, *Head of Christ*, c. 1648. Oil on oak panel, 9.8 x 8.5 inches. Gemäldegalerie, Berlin. Public domain. Credit: Sailko. Source:https://commons.wikimedia.org/wiki/File:Rembrandt_Harmensz._van_Rijn_048.jpg

(Pg. 84) Rembrandt van Rijn, *Christ in the Storm on the Lake of Galilee*, 1633. Oil on canvas, 63 x 50.4 inches. Currently stolen from Isabella Stewart Gardner Museum, Boston. Public domain. Source: https://commons.wikimedia.org/wiki/File:Rembrandt_Christ_in_the_Storm_on_the_Lake_of_Galilee.jpg

(Pg. 93) Katsushika Hokusai, *The Great Wave Off Kanagawa*, first printed 1826–33. Color woodblock print from *Thirty-Six Views of Mount Fuji*. Public domain. Source: https://commons.wikimedia.org/wiki/File:Great_Wave_off_Kanagawa2.jpg

(Pg. 103) Henryk Siemiradzki, *Christ in the House of Martha and Mary*, 1886. Oil on canvas, size unavailable. Russian Museum, St. Petersburg, Russia. Public domain. Source: http://www.wikiart.org/en/henryk-siemiradzki/christ-in-the-house-of-martha-and-mary

(Pg. 116) Paul Landowski (designer), *Christ the Redeemer*, 1922–31. Reinforced concrete and soapstone, 98 ft. Corcovado, Rio de Janeiro, Brazil. Public domain. Credit: Artyominc. Source: https://commons.wikimedia.org/wiki/File:Christ_on_Corcovado_mountain.JPG

(Pg. 118) *Christ the Redeemer* statue on Corcovado Mountain stands 98 feet tall on a 26-foot pedestal, his arms outstretched a grand 92 feet wide. It is made of reinforced concrete and covered with thousands of soapstone mosaic tiles. Credit: Dkoukoul. Source: https://commons.wikimedia.org/wiki/File:Christ_the_Redeemer_statue_at_Corcovado.JPG

(Pg. 125) Ford Madox Brown, *Jesus Washing Peter's Feet*, 1852–6. Oil on canvas, 46 x 52 ½ inches. Tate Gallery, London, UK. Public domain. Source: http://www.wikiart.org/en/ford-madox-brown/jesus-washing-peter-s-feet-1876 - close

(Pg. 135) Ford Madox Brown, *Pretty Baa-Lambs,* 1851–59. Oil on panel, 30 x 24 inches. Birmingham Museum and Art Gallery, Birmingham, UK. Public domain. Source: https://commons.wikimedia.org/wiki/File:Ford_Madox_Brown_-_Pretty_Baa-Lambs_-_Google_Art_Project.jpg

(Pg. 138) Pietro Perugino, *The Crucifixion with the Virgin, Saint John, Saint Jerome, and Saint Mary Magdalene,* 1482-85. Oil on panel transferred to canvas, 52 ¾ x 65 x 2 ⅞ inches. Andrew W. Mellon Collection, National Gallery of Art, Washington DC. Public domain. Source: NGA Open Access.

(Pg. 141) Leonardo da Vinci, Leonardo, testa di Cristo, c. 1494. Chalk and pencil on paper. 15.7 x 12.6 inches. Pinacoteca di Brera. Milan. Public Domain. Source: https://commons.wikimedia.org/wiki/File:Leonardo,_testa_di_cristo,_1494_circa,_pinacoteca_di_brera.jpg

(Pg. 146) Jodie Marie Anne Richardson Traugott (jm-ART), *Crucifixion,* 2013. Digital photograph. http://fineartamerica.com/featured/crucifixion-jodie-marie-anne-richardson-traugott---aka-jm-art-.html. Photographed in Santa Fe, NM, Cathedral Basilica of Saint Francis of Assisi. Used by permission of the artist.

(Pg. 179) Rogier van der Weyden, *The Descent from the Cross,* 1435–38. Oil on panel, 86.6 x 103.1 inches. Prado Museum, Madrid, Spain. Public domain. Source: https://commons.wikimedia.org/wiki/File:Weyden-descendimiento-prado-Ca-1435.jpg

(Pg. 187) *Descent from the Cross* (detail: Stabat Mater (Mary), left; tears) Public domain. Source: https://commons.wikimedia.org/wiki/File:Weyden,_Rogier_van_der_-_Descent_from_the_Cross_-_Detail_women_(left).jpg

(Pg. 197) William-Adolphe Bouguereau, *The Holy Women at the Tomb of Christ,* 1890. Oil on canvas, dimensions unavailable. Koninkiljk Museum voor Schone Kunsten, Antwerp Belgium. Source: © Lukas - Art in Flanders VZW / Photo: Hugo Maertens / Bridgeman Images

(Pg. 211) William-Adolphe Bouguereau, *The Virgin of the Lilies,* 1899. Oil on canvas, dimensions unavailable. Private collection. Source: Image courtesy of the Art Renewal Center ® www.artrenewal.org

(Pg. 214) *Christ Pantocrator* (Christ Blessing) icon, sixth century. Encaustic on panel, 33 x 18 inches. St. Catherine's Monastery, Mount Sinai. Public domain. Source: https://commons.wikimedia.org/wiki/File:Spas_vsederzhitel_sinay.jpg

(Pg. 217) Courtyard of the Church of the Multiplication, Tabgha, Israel. Photo by David Shankbone. (Use of this photo does not in any way endorse the work of this author.) Source: https://commons.wikimedia.org/wiki/File:Courtyard_of_the_Church_of_the_Multiplication_in_Tabgha_by_David_Shankbone.jpg

(Pg. 222) Byzantine mosaic of the Loaves and Fishes, c. A.D. 480. Church of the Multiplication, Tabgha, Israel. Public domain. Source: https://commons.wikimedia.org/wiki/File:Brotvermehrungskirche_BW_3.JPG

(Pg. 237) Tiffany Glass and Decorating Co., Christ and the Apostles, triptych window, circa 1890. Leaded and enameled stained glass, side panels 80 ¾ x 34 ⅝ inches, middle panel 80 ¾ x 39 ⅛ inches. Richard H. Driehaus Gallery of Stained Glass at the Navy Pier, Chicago IL. Source: https://commons.wikimedia.org/wiki/File:Christ_and_the_Apostles_-_Tiffany_Glass_%26_Decorating_Company,_c._1890.JPG

(Pg. 246) Pieter Bruegel, *The Harvesters,* 1565. Oil on panel, 46.9 x 68.8 inches. Metropolitan Museum of Art, New York City. Public domain. Source: https://commons.wikimedia.org/wiki/File:Pieter_Bruegel_the_Elder-_The_Harvesters_-_Google_Art_Project.jpg

(Pg. 249) Pieter Bruegel, *The Harvesters,* 1565. Lower Left Detail of Men with Scythe. Metropolitan Museum of Art, New York City. Public domain. Source: https://commons.wikimedia.org/wiki/File:Pieter_Bruegel_the_Elder-_The_Harvesters_-_Google_Art_Project-x0-y1.jpg

(Pg. 257) John August Swanson, *Festival of Lights,* 2000. Serigraph, 30.75 x 24 inches. © 2000 www.JohnAugustSwanson.com. Used by permission of the artist. Source: http://www.johnaugustswanson.com/ImagesUpload/festival_of_lights_450.jpg

(Pg. 261) Raphael, *Eight Apostles,* c. 1514, Red chalk drawing, 3 3/16 x 9 1/8 inches. Woodner Collection, National Gallery of Art, Washington DC. Public domain. Source: NGA Open Access

ACKNOWLEDGMENTS

All praise and glory to God the Father whose guiding hand I could feel in both little and large ways throughout the writing process. Each morning was ripe with new possibilities, as I would rise before the dawn, to be still and listen for the pleasure of hearing his voice leading my thoughts towards new discoveries. I thank him for the strength and insight I needed to make this journey and for all the little surprises along the way. I often felt myself like Henry Tanner's *Banjo Lesson*, sitting on the Father's lap as he gently guided me towards each new discovery.

I continue to thank my parents for the very strong Bible knowledge and a love of learning they gave me. My mother who has been my ultimate champion; who taught me the art of storytelling and who listened to my ideas for this book daily; and my father, now passed, who is still my picture of a faith that never waivers and a love for God that surpasses all understanding.

I have made many new friends since my first publication and I would like to thank all of those who helped me with their prayers, encouraging words, speaking opportunities and individual Bible expertise: Pastor Karin Aulds Albaugh, Pastor Charlene Barnes, Richard Beck, Judy Bergeson, Carol and Roger Boyd, Beverly Butts, K. Rex Butts, Tanya Burnham, Allen Carr, Shane Coffman, Juanita Davis, John Dobbs, Thomas Dockery, Charlotte Dodson, Scott Elliot, Brandon Fredenburg, Mary Hampton, Marilyn Harrington, John Mark Hicks, Peter Horne, Janice Tharp Garrison, Boyd Goodson, Lynn and Jerry Jones, Leo Kerlick, Stanley Kerlick, Anne Langston, D'Esta Love, Mark Love, Richard and JeannaLynn May, Pastor Surekha Nelavala, Adam and Sarah Nettesheim, Mike O'Neal, Jerry Pennybaker, Lori and Andre Risse, Jerry Rushford, Will Spina, Nancy Saltzman, Jeanie Wilbur and Roger Woods.

I am thankful for my work family at Frederick Community College and Mount Saint Mary's University and all my students who provide me with strength daily. Specifically I am indebted to Jan Holly, Wendell Poindexter, and Dave Moreland for giving me the opportunity to develop this synthesis of the arts in the classroom and giving me the courage to become an Art teacher. I also want to thank Paula Chipman and John Wickelgren who have supported me in various ways through encouraging words and filling in for me when I have been away from my post.

Special thanks to my writing coach David Hazard who saw the possibilities of this project and encouraged me to write this second book by once again becoming the guiding hand with me throughout the process. Having someone of his experience to nurture my ideas into a completed book was essential and for that I am again most grateful. Thanks also to Arin Murphy-Hiscock who helped me with her keen eye and heart for editing. She was just the right balance of encourager and critic that I needed to give birth to this second book project. Thank you to Peter Gloege for his hand in the design of the beautiful cover of this book and for all the special touches he so painstakingly administered inside to "dress up" the contents of my thoughts.

And finally I thank God for my husband Simon who is always with me on this journey, quietly observing, offering advice when asked and allowing me the time and space to nurture my dream of connecting people to God thru the Arts.

ABOUT THE AUTHOR

Jennifer Rundlett, founder of God thru the Arts ministries, maintains a presence in the community with her active lecture and concert series highlighting the spiritual connections throughout the arts. Author of *My Dancing Day: Reflections of the Incarnation in Art and Music*, she regularly posts devotional blogs on God thru the Arts at http://www.jrundlett.wordpress.com and has been a speaker at the Pepperdine University Bible Lectures in Malibu CA, Tulsa Workshop in Tulsa OK, David Lipscomb University *Summer Celebration* in Nashville TN, Rochester College *Streaming* in Rochester Hills Michigan and Fort Detrick Prayer Breakfast in Frederick Maryland.

A native Californian, Jennifer received her Bachelor Degree in Music from California State University at Northridge where she studied with many of the working studio musicians of the Los Angeles area. She studied at Peabody Conservatory of Music in Baltimore where she studied with Tim Day Principal Flute of Baltimore Symphony and later Robert Willoughby Principal Flute of the Cincinnati Symphony. Upon receiving her Masters of Music, Jennifer then went on to study in England with Trevor Wye at the Royal Northern College of Music where she received a Post Graduate Diploma in Flute Performance.

Jennifer has been teaching flute to children and adults of all ages and levels of experience for over 20 years. She is an active member of the faculty of Frederick Community College and Mount Saint Mary's University where in addition to maintaining her flute studio, she teaches "Music History & Appreciation," "Introduction to the Creative Arts," "Survey of World Music," and is the director of the FCC Flute choir. An active recitalist in the Mid-Atlantic region she has recently appeared as soloist with the National String Symphonia and enjoys playing and performing with the Wedgewood Flute Quartet.

She is also the coordinator and administrator of the annual Shields Music Scholarship competition that awards approximately 40 prizes to young musicians for their tuition to study music at Frederick Community College. Jennifer is currently serving as the Interim Music Program Manager at FCC since Fall 2014.